Ordained Ministry in
The United Methodist Church

Ordained Ministry in
The United Methodist Church

William B. Lawrence

General Board of Higher Education and Ministry
The United Methodist Church
Nashville, Tennessee

The General Board of Higher Education and Ministry leads and serves The United Methodist Church in the recruitment, preparation, nurture, education, and support of Christian leaders—lay and clergy—for the work of making disciples of Jesus Christ for the transformation of the world. Its vision is that a new generation of Christian leaders will commit boldly to Jesus Christ and be characterized by intellectual excellence, moral integrity, spiritual courage, and holiness of heart and life.

The General Board of Higher Education and Ministry of The United Methodist Church is the church's agency for educational, institutional, and ministerial leadership. It serves as an advocate for the intellectual life of the church. The Board's mission embodies the Wesleyan tradition of commitment to the education of laypersons and ordained persons by providing access to higher education for all persons.

ISBN 978-0-938162-69-8

Produced by the Office of Interpretation

Manufactured in the United States of America

Contents

Introduction

God must have a keen sense of humor. Or, at the very least, God must have an endless capacity to be amused.

Consider the dizzying array of the world's religions. All claim to do their business in the name of God. And each seems to create an entertaining assortment of teachings, tenets, and traditions. Some of them are nearly comic, like the acceptance of an ordained priesthood in the Anglican branch of Christianity in which male clergy are comfortably addressed with the gender-based title *Father*, while female clergy cause consternation among traditionalists who cannot seem to address ordained women by the equally gender-based title *Mother*. Others among the world's religions have teachings, tenets, and traditions that are deeply tragic, such as requiring human sacrifice, launching military crusades, or honoring suicide raids. And most religions are so different from others that their believers have found multiple barriers to communicating with one another about their commitments and convictions.

There is not even any consistency in the ways religions get their names.

Some were derived directly from their principles of belief or practices of living. *Taoism*, for instance, literally means the path or the way of life; it was built upon values of compassion, moderation, and humility. *Islam* actually means "submission to God and to God's will," as it is taught in the Qur'an; so to be a Muslim is to submit oneself to the patterns of prayer and practice that are willed by God to be proper for adherents.

Other religions acquired their institutional identity from the personal name of the founder or authority. Confucianism was developed upon the philosophical and ethical system of the sixth-century teacher named Confucius. Buddhism offers a way to enlightenment that is traced to a fifth-century contemplative figure whose adopted nickname was the Buddha. Christianity is identified by its central conviction that Jesus of Nazareth was the awaited Messiah, or Anointed One, or Christ, whose coming was prophesied in Israel.

Within the broad base of these mammoth, global religions are the branches, sects, and denominations that developed their own brands.

Some Christian sects retained the names of their founders. Lutherans trace their heritage and beliefs to Martin Luther, who launched the Protestant Reformation in the sixteenth century, and to the body of doctrine that emerged from his teachings. Mennonites trace their lineage to another Reformer of the sixteenth century, Menno Simons, who took a different slant on the basic impulses of the Reformation. Mar Thoma Christians, whose roots are in India, rely on the tradition that the apostle Thomas overcame his doubts about the resurrection of Jesus and embarked on a mission to India, where he established their church.

Other Christian groups stake their claims not on persons but on patterns and practices. There are various types of Baptists. What they share is a view of being fundamentally formed into congregations of individuals who freely associate with one another and offer personal confessions of faith that they mark by a rite of baptism— usually by a full-body immersion. The Orthodox, as their name literally suggests, insist that true Christianity is a matter of correctly glorifying or praising God through proper worship based on proper beliefs; within that broad self-understanding, they are identified by their national or ethnic boundaries as Greek, Russian, Armenian, or some other Orthodox. And Roman Catholics, as their name suggests, see themselves as the one truly "universal" church with its headquarters in Rome.

Each of these bodies has defined its own systems for identifying, recruiting, training, certifying, and deploying persons for present and future leadership. Buddhist masters and monks train the next cohort of masters and monks. Baptist congregations operate independently, and freely choose those whom they will call as leaders or pastors, freely decide whether to accept women as well as men (or persons whose sexual orientation is hetero, homo, or bi) in leadership, and freely determine whether specialized education (or the lack of it) satisfies their spiritual standards and intellectual expectations for training.

Most, but not all, of these religious traditions refer to ordination or ordained ministry as a category of authorization for leadership. Almost all Christian bodies have developed an ordination process of some kind. Yet there are exceptions. Quakers are generally accepted as belonging to the large family of Christian sects or denominations, but they have no ordained ministers and no professional cohort of leaders at all. Presbyterians, Baptists, and Methodists all have categories of ordained ministry, and all of them refer to certain persons as deacons and elders. But they do not all understand those titles to refer to the same kinds of ordained ministry.

Mormons—who may or may not be counted as Christians depending on one's point of view theologically—have "elders," but they tend to be young persons who are beginning some form of lay mission work early in their careers, not entering upon a lifetime of pastoral or professional ministry through ordination.

Islam does not ordain its imams, but they are chosen with care to lead prayers and to preach. Judaism has a long tradition of ordained leaders, stretching back to the ordination of Moses' brother, Aaron. Described in Leviticus 8, Aaron was ordained in a broad and bloody ritual that lasted seven days. It certainly inaugurated the priesthood with its cult of prayer and sacrifice in a grand style. Today rabbis in Judaism are ordained, but not as priests in the tradition of Aaron. Nor are they granted their authorizations for rabbinical leadership through weeklong festivals featuring animal sacrifice. Rather, they are ordained in prayerful rituals to teach the law of God and to make discerning judgments about applying the law of God to human circumstances.

All of this is to suggest that a brief attempt to answer the question, what is ordained ministry? should be undertaken with a considerable sense of modesty. The terms *ordain* and *ordination* have many different connotations and meanings with regard to religious leadership. An ordained rabbi leading a Jewish congregation may have more in common professionally with an unordained imam than with an ordained Roman Catholic priest. Yet all sects and cults and religious cultures will have considerably different understandings of ordination and leadership because of their remarkably diverse traditions.

One cannot explore an answer to the question, what is ordained ministry? without an awareness of the extraordinary range of ideas that attach themselves to the concept. Some rabbis, for instance, chafe at the expectations of persons in their synagogues who have heard their Catholic and Protestant neighbors describe with great appreciation the care that their priests and pastors offered during an illness of a family member. These rabbis understand themselves to be ordained as teachers and interpreters of Jewish law, not as pastoral care givers or comforters who visit the sick. Other professionals and perhaps some volunteers in the congregation should do that. Nevertheless, rabbis who understand themselves as being ordained to study and to teach sometimes feel pressured to make hospital calls and nursing home visits. In the end, they may do so for secular rather than for religious reasons.

Perhaps God has a sense of humor about all of these complexities and complications. We human beings and our institutions may have a little more difficulty with them than humor can tolerate. Often political and ideological issues intrude on the matter.

In countries with an officially established religion, for example, national laws can be written to exercise some control over the structures of religious leadership, the authorizations that may be granted to leaders within religions, the educational criteria that must be met to be ordained or certified, and even the places of service to which persons may be assigned. An imam in Turkey, which is overwhelmingly Muslim but officially tolerant of all religions, will be assigned to a mosque by a national governing body. A Methodist in Malaysia, a nation whose official religion is Islam, may be free to exercise religious leadership within his or her own constituency but not be permitted to recruit persons from other bodies into the Methodist Church or be publicly identified as a Methodist. Indeed, a Methodist bishop in Malaysia told me a few years ago that his driver's license listed him as a Muslim. He said that he has tried to have the designation changed, but his government's bureaucracy seems to lack the capacity to do so. The political system in the State of Israel has a formal mechanism for defining who is a Jew, preferring not to leave that determination to individual rabbis or congregations or random associations of theological assemblies. And the political system in Great Britain, with its officially established Church of England, technically controls the appointments of bishops and archbishops as the ordained leaders of their dioceses.

In countries without an officially established religion, the situation is no less complex or confusing.

The United States of America, where the first constitutional protection in the Bill of Rights guarantees that Congress shall make no law to provide for the establishment of religion or to prohibit the free exercise thereof, has a bewildering array of complications regarding ordained ministry. On a national level, for example, it has been determined that the country's military personnel will be served by chaplains from various religious traditions. On the one hand, the federal government retains the final authority to decide who will be deployed as a chaplain with a military unit. On the other hand, the federal government permits the various religious bodies in the land a considerable amount of freedom to decide when candidates for the chaplaincy have met the requirements for full ordination or authorization in their separate traditions.

The federal government has also determined, through the statutes and regulations associated with the income tax code, that "ordained ministers" have certain benefits that are not available to most other persons. A notable example of this is the provision that lets an ordained person's employer (whether that employer is a religious body, such as a church, or a secular entity, such as a university) designate a portion of that individual's compensation as "housing allowance," which might potentially reduce the person's income tax obligations. It may be that anyone who claims such a benefit could be required to prove that she or he is an ordained minister under the polity of some established religious body, but the government is loath to violate the Constitution by determining which religions and which forms of the ordained ministry are legitimate. That judgment is left to the organized religious bodies themselves.

Federal laws and regulations are not the end of the challenges to an easy understanding of ordained ministry in a country with no established religion.

Each of the 50 states has considerable latitude in defining the systems that control definitions of marriage and determinations about who may sign the licenses that create marriages. Many states require that the person performing a marriage be either a secular authority (e.g., a judge or civil magistrate) or an ordained minister. But states are either ill-equipped or ill-advised to answer the question, who is an ordained minister? So some simply follow the principle of self-declaration, and they accept the notion that if you say that you are ordained, then you are approved to conduct (and sign licenses for) weddings. Others require some kind of documentation from a denomination or a religious body that is proof of one's ordination. Securing such a document is not necessarily that difficult. For a charge of $25 plus a processing fee, one can acquire a certificate of ordination within a week from the "American Fellowship Church." As an alternative, instantaneously and for free, one can receive certificates of ordination from the "Universal Life Church Monastery," the "Church of Spiritual Humanism," and the "Church of the Latter-Day Dude."[1] They will probably enable almost anyone to conduct marriage ceremonies in any of the 50 states.

Oddly enough, as easy as it may be to become an ordained minister for the purpose of creating a legal marriage, there is no state in the country that permits an ordained minister to dissolve a legal marriage. It is a curiosity of our constitutionally secure religious freedom that ordination confers the authority to establish this one fundamental and binding sort of legal contract but does not confer the authority to terminate it.

In the end, it may be clearer who ordained ministers are and what ordained ministers can do in countries with officially established religions than it is in one country where an official religion establishment is prohibited.

So it is immensely complicated to answer in a general sense the question, what is ordained ministry? It will be complex enough to answer the question in the context of

Methodism, and that is the purpose of this book. Some basic boundaries can be established quickly. Even the name *Methodist* creates a distinctive characteristic. The denomination is not named for its founding figure, some specific liturgical action, or some central point of doctrine. Rather, the name *Methodist* comes from an epithet tossed at the early adherents of a movement that used means or methods of discipline for structuring activities, making choices, and practicing faith.

In The United Methodist Church today, the path to ordained ministry involves a complex method of decisions by numerous bodies, no one of which has complete control of the process, but many of which have sole authority to stop the ordination process at any of several points. And the method that the church uses to reach the moment when one is ordained by a bishop has enough bewildering aspects to discourage even the most gifted and dedicated candidate for ordination. For example, in The United Methodist Church, it is technically true that only a bishop may ordain, but the church's bishops are the only persons who are technically prohibited from voting on who may be ordained. And that is just one of the peculiarities within the method that United Methodists use to ordain their leaders.

Another frequently misunderstood peculiarity involves the nature of ordination itself. A Methodist who is ordained holds an "office" and is elected to an "order" either as an elder or a deacon. A United Methodist deacon is ordained for ministries of word and service. A United Methodist elder is ordained for ministries of word, service, sacrament, and order. Deacons are ordained to assist in the sacraments but not to preside in administering them. Elders are ordained to order the life of the church, including the ordained ministries of the denomination, but they share that authority with deacons, who are not actually ordained to carry such a responsibility. And specific ministries for which they are ordained as deacons and elders may be fulfilled by persons who are not ordained to either office, provided those persons are appointed by bishops to local churches or other specific places of ministry.

While all of this may seem strange, if not downright odd, there is a methodical logic to it. The ordained ministry in Methodism is a set of offices which are occupied by persons who have been designated by the church to fulfill those offices for the sake of the church. To be granted such an office and to enter such an order is to be authorized by the church — in this case, by The United Methodist Church — to conduct certain ministerial functions that the church has mandated. Both deacons and elders are ordained to the ministry of the Word, for example. This does not mean that they are the only ones who can preach the Word, for Methodism has always had provision for laypersons to preach and teach the Word of God. But it does mean that those who are ordained have been designated by the church, have been given a mandate by the church, and will be held accountable by the church, for properly conducting the ministry of the Word.

Hence, ordination must always be understood as entry into an office that one occupies, not as an identity that one has been granted or that one owns. An individual who is ordained does not undergo a transformation of human character. Following ordination, one is the same human being as she or he was before the ritual. Becoming ordained, in short, does not involve becoming some other form of being. There are Christian religious traditions in which that claim is made, but the Methodist tradition is not one of them. When a service of ordination ends and when the new ordinands process out of the worship center, their hair may be pressed down a bit from the bishop's hands that were laid upon them, and the smiles on their faces may be excessively wide at the realization that a journey of many years has come to a point of culmination. But, at the conclusion of the process, every ordinand will remain blessed with the same gifts, burdened with the same limitations, driven by the same hopes, and drained by the same frailties that dwelt in their souls before the service began.

Moreover, within Methodism, ordained ministry is not something that belongs to the individual. To be ordained is not to acquire a status that one lacked prior to ordination. To be ordained is to enter into an office that belongs to the church. It is a kind of tenancy. One occupies the office as long as the church deems it appropriate to be the case. One wears the symbols of the office as long as the church chooses to grant that privilege. Ordination is not an entitlement that one secures by achieving a specified educational level, by successfully completing a series of examinations, by enduring a grueling process of inquiry over several years, by undergoing repeated periods of supervision at the hands of other church authorities, or by receiving lavish praise from persons with whom one engages in acts of ministry. One never owns one's ordination. It always belongs to the church.

Ordained ministry is not the only form of ministerial leadership in Methodism. Since the earliest days of the Methodist movement and throughout its history, almost all forms of ministry have been legitimately performed by persons who were not ordained. Lay preachers have been a fixture in Methodist life. A host of positions has been occupied by laity, some with considerably more real power and control than ordained ministers could claim. The most influential leaders in small-membership churches during the late nineteenth century and early twentieth, for instance, might have been superintendents of the Sunday schools or the presidents of the boards of trustees. Plenty of ordained ministers appointed to be pastors of local churches have learned church polity the hard way when they discovered all the means by which local church laity had far more authority than they in certain matters. Funds controlled by a local church's unit of the United Methodist Women (or its predecessor bodies such as the Women's Society of Christian Service or the Wesleyan Service Guild) were not subject to control by the official board, administrative board, church council, or any other governing body of the congregation, and certainly could not be disbursed by the authority of the pastor, no matter how many bishops' hands had been laid upon the person's head at the time of ordination.

So ordained ministry in Methodism is an office that one occupies; it is a position of leadership with clear limits on the ways it can be used to lead; and it is one of many offices the church has established to achieve its mission. United Methodists have created sets of complex, interlocking systems for identifying, recruiting, educating, authorizing, training, electing, assigning, appointing, and evaluating leaders, including those who are ordained. Those systems are often confusing to average Methodists, and they are utterly bewildering to people who have minimal familiarity with the denomination.

Although it seems a relatively basic matter of vocabulary that ordained ministers are clergy and that people who are not ordained are laity, those definitions do not necessarily hold in the arcane jargon of United Methodism. Certain categories of people who are not ordained—licensed and appointed local pastors, to be specific—are counted as clergy within the church's annual conferences. So are "provisional members" of United Methodist annual conferences, who are not ordained[2] but may be "commissioned" for ministry. In short, the terms *ordained* and *clergy* are not necessarily parallel and certainly are not to be understood as synonyms.

Notwithstanding all of the things that cause confusion for answering the question, what is ordained ministry? it is clear that ordained ministry is a prescription for one way to live the life of faith. And among Christians, particularly among people called Methodists, ordained ministry can be the most satisfying, fulfilling, energizing, engaging, challenging, and transforming way of life one could ever ponder. For it offers, by the grace of God through the church, an office within which one can exercise leadership on behalf of the church in every corner of the world, in every aspect of human existence, in an encounter with every structure of human society, in the midst of every facet of existence, at the edge of every boundary of life. Many professions and careers can allow similar access, perhaps. But none does so with the full range of opportunity that ordained ministry can afford, and none does so with the full authorization of the church for bearing the means of God's grace to touch every human need.

There are a lot of things that look like ordained ministry. But only the real thing is empowered by the church to deliver the grace that it claims.

Notes

1. Jane Hodges, "Chapel Bound: Getting Ordained Online," *Wall Street Journal*, June 12, 2008, D4.
2. Unless they were previously ordained in another denomination and are currently in the process of entering into clergy membership of The United Methodist Church. This complication will be addressed later.

CHAPTER 1

The Partner of All Conflicts

In a sense, Methodists have been trying to answer the question, what is ordained ministry? ever since Methodism began. From its start as an effort to bring about spiritual renewal within the established Church of England in the eighteenth century, to its emergence as a network of independent church bodies that now claim more than 70 million members in countries around the globe, Methodism has been discussing and debating ordained ministry.

Conflicts erupted between the founding Wesley brothers, John and Charles, over whether the growing movement they launched should have its own ordained ministry. That dispute did not end until after Charles had died and the American colonists' revolutionary war had ended, with American Methodists living as citizens of an independent nation.

In different eras and regions, different branches of the Methodist family reached opposing answers to questions about ordination and ordained ministry.

Historical Foundations

Shortly after its formation in the 1780s, the Methodist Episcopal Church in the United States of America decided that it would have three orders of ministry: deacons, elders, and bishops.[1] British Methodists decided they would have an ordained ministry but would not have bishops. Methodist Protestants in the United States in the 1820s, reaching a conclusion that they wanted a church without a bishop in a country without a king, formed a new denomination to insist on it. Methodists in South Africa decided to have bishops but only for specified terms of office. Today's United Methodists, primarily located in the United States but widely dispersed in many countries around the world, have bishops who are elected for life but are subject to a mandatory retirement age.

The other offices of ordained ministry have been inconsistently identified by various Methodist bodies. Methodist Protestants and United Brethren did not bother with a sequential ordination of deacon and elder. The African Methodist Episcopal Church ordains people sequentially as deacon and elder, remaining today in the Anglican pattern that most (but not all) Methodists adopted. United Methodists, who maintained a pattern of sequential ordination that endured through numerous denominational mergers, decided in 1996 to put the offices of deacon and elder into separate, rather than sequential, orders of ministry.

Issues concerning the structure of the ordained ministry are not the only divisive topics. And no one should think that these or other matters of dispute have been settled. After all, every aspect of the way that ordained ministry is structured in The United Methodist Church today has a long, complex, and theologically defensible description.

John Wesley was himself ordained in the Church of England, first as a deacon in 1725, then as a presbyter (i.e., elder or priest) in 1728. The system that he knew, the one in which he was nurtured, and the one in which he received his official credentials for ministry, had a sequential approach. A candidate for ordination, having earned a bachelor's degree and having successfully passed an examination by a bishop, would be ordained deacon. Then, having pursued a master's degree and having successfully passed a second examination by the bishop after a probationary period of two years, the candidate would be ordained elder.[2]

Ord. for Wesley.

Through the years that followed, his thinking about ordination was influenced by many factors. His brother Charles argued that only a bishop could ordain someone to the ministry. His readings in ecumenical theology led him to think that anyone who was ordained as a presbyter (elder or priest) had the same scriptural authority as a bishop in the matter. In the end, his resistance to authorize ordinations for the Methodist movement crumbled in the face of practical realities. American Methodism was developing and expanding in a newly independent nation. British Methodism was growing as a separate, dissenting movement. If Methodists were to have access to the sacraments and if Methodism was to have an institutional future, ordained ministers would be needed.

So Wesley authorized ordination, and he adhered to the sequential pattern that was familiar to him. From 1784 onward, Methodists were ordained deacon and then ordained elder. The two ministries were not necessarily distinguished from each other by substance as much as by sequence. Francis Asbury was ordained deacon and elder on successive days, and on the third day he rose to the rank of superintendent or (as he soon called himself) bishop. A deacon was intended to be under supervised probation until he was ordained as an elder, but the two ministries were chronologically separated facets of the same authorization. In the mainstream of American Methodism, that pattern remained for more than 200 years.

But other patterns surfaced in various Methodist groups and in Methodist-related bodies. The Methodist Protestant Church dispensed not only with the office of bishop but also with the order of deacon and had only one ordination, that of elder. The United Brethren also ordained persons only to the office of elder. The Evangelical Association followed the sequential pattern of ordaining deacons and elders, but at least in some cases the sequencing was like that of Asbury's ordinations, on consecutive days.[3]

These differences were woven by twentieth-century developments into what is now the structure of the ordained ministry in The United Methodist Church. A reunion of Northern and Southern Methodists together with the Methodist Protestants in 1939 included an affirmation of the sequential process with deacons and elders. A 1946 merger of the Evangelical Church and the Church of the United Brethren created the Evangelical United Brethren (EUB), which ordained only elders.[4] In 1968, when The Methodist Church and the EUB merged, the sequential ordination of deacons and elders prevailed as the established system.

And so it remained until 1996, when the General Conference of The United Methodist Church eliminated the sequential ordering of ministry and replaced it with a substantive ordering of ministry. The Order of Deacons was designated for persons authorized to preach the Word and to engage in service. The Order of Elders was designated for persons who are authorized to preach the Word, engage in service, preside at the sacraments, and order the church. Both deacons and elders are now understood as fully ordained ministers in the church, and both hold membership within their respective annual conferences. But they are now understood as belonging to two separate orders of ministry, with distinct authorizations and with different mechanisms for entering into specific forms of professional ministry that are consistent with their senses of vocations and with their ecclesiastical authority as granted by ordination.

It is important to note that United Methodism and its predecessor denominations have had commissions or committees conducting studies of the ordained ministry almost continuously for nearly seventy years. Arguments continue over whether deacons should have authority to administer—not merely assist in administering—the sacraments. Disputes arise over whether persons whose ministry of the Word will be in the very narrow confines of academic scholarship and university teaching should be ordained elder or should be limited to the office of deacon.

Inseparable from these conflicts are lingering divisions about gender. With only a few rare exceptions in most of Methodist history, women were restricted from ordained ministry and have been limited to certain specific forms of ministry. Women remain a far larger percentage of United Methodist deacons and a far smaller percentage of United Methodist elders than equitable roles for ministerial leadership would suggest.

Inseparable, too, from these conflicts are the multiple forms of credentialing that United Methodists struggle to identify as normative for ordination. How much education, at what level of graduate degree, in what academic disciplines, demonstrating what theological competencies, and from what institutions, should be required for ordination into the ministry of The United Methodist Church? What standards of psychological health, measured by what standardized systems of measurement, reviewed by what sorts of credentialed professionals, and revealed to whom in ecclesiastical authority, should be required for ordination into the ministry of The United Methodist Church? What practices in spiritual formation, what sensitivities about interpersonal harassment (sexual, ethnic, racial, economic), and what skills in organizational leadership, should be required for ordination into the ministry of The United Methodist Church?

In the twenty-first century, these are among many lively matters of discussion, dispute, and debate. Conflicts over them abound. And these conflicts about ordained ministry become partnered with every other divisive issue in the life of the denomination. No one would have to peek very far below the surface in The United Methodist Church today to discover that there is a lot of conflict in the denomination. Disagreements are rampant about the causes of, and the solutions to, declines in church membership since the middle of the twentieth century. Debates are rising over the ways to allocate fewer available funds for more emerging needs. Differences are reaching into every corner of church structure about the proper organizational pattern for fulfilling the church's mission in the twenty-first century. Disputes are raging over an array of moral, political, and social questions—homosexuality, immigration, abortion, and health care among them.

Conflicts Linked to Social Issues

Some of those disagreements resonate with political

and social arguments in the larger society. And almost all of them have been linked to disputes about the role or responsibilities of ordained ministry.

In the spring of 2010, when a decisive vote was about to be taken by the U.S. House of Representatives on a bill to reform health care, many United Methodists (some with shock, others with awe) heard the Speaker of the House thank "The United Methodist Church" for supporting the movement toward health-care reform. Various church leaders—and not a few bishops among them—scrambled to issue statements responding to the Speaker's words. They attempted to clarify, or to correct or create some distance from, her words. It was an unexpected moment when the denomination found itself in such a prominent national arena on the topic of health care, and it exposed the differences of opinion that exist in the church on that issue. It has come as a surprise to many United Methodists, for instance, that the church has officially taken the position that "health care is a basic human right" (*The Book of Discipline*, ¶ 162V, p. 117).

Partnered with that controversial statement is a question: should ordained ministers teach or preach about such things in their work?

More prominent among the divisive issues in the church is homosexuality, a topic that has been openly discussed since the formation of the united church in 1968 and has been the most conflicted issue in the Methodist connection for about three decades. Like abortion, which is probably the second most divisive topic for debates in the church, it is a matter that tends toward absolute points of view. Some United Methodists insist that human beings with a homosexual orientation must be fully and inclusively affirmed in the life of the church or, they say, the church is not a community of grace. Other United Methodists insist that homosexuals have to be recognized by the church as gripped by a moral evil from which they must be delivered or, they say, the church has made an unacceptable accommodation to sin.

In its own way, the denomination has embraced a number of absolutist positions on the topic of homosexuality, while appearing to compromise. The applicable statement in the Social Principles of The United Methodist Church attempts to hold multiple points of view that may be in conflict with each other: we are all sexual beings, we are all individuals of sacred worth, and the only sorts of sexual relations that will be affirmed are those that occur in the covenant of heterosexual marriage (*The Book of Discipline*, ¶ 161F, p. 103). Every United Methodist can find at least one of those three clauses acceptable, but it remains doubtful whether all United Methodists are content with those three clauses as an expression of their own perspectives.

From what perspective, if any, should ordained ministers teach or preach about this in their work?

In the late nineteenth century and the early twentieth, beverage alcohol provided the church with an issue for decisive battle. A temperance movement within American Methodism formed alliances with the interests of groups such as the Anti-Saloon League, helped in campaigns to bring about a "dry" nation, found support for shifting to the use of unfermented grape juice in Holy Communion, constructed a building in the nation's capital that offered an ideal location for keeping an eye on the Supreme Court as well as lobbying the Congress, and helped pass both the Eighteenth Amendment to the Constitution and the Volstead Act to establish Prohibition as the law of the land.

Plenty of ordained ministers preached and taught about that in their work. Indeed, they were held accountable to a life of abstinence by church law.

Health care, homosexuality, abortion, and temperance have been subjects of significant debate within the church. As disputed and divisive as these issues were (or are), none of them has led to an actual schism in the church. Uncounted parishioners may have flocked to or fled from the church on the basis of such social or political positions. But none of these issues has yet caused a fracturing of the church into fragments. Indeed, even the long, intense contest over the matter of homosexuality has not affected United Methodism the way similar debates have fragmented other denominations. Unlike the Episcopal Church in the United States, which has had several diocesan bodies vote to leave the national church and seek other paths to relate to the global Anglican communion, no whole conferences (and few, if any congregations) in United Methodism have yet attempted to secede from the connectional church. It certainly could happen. But, at least on these matters of dispute, it has not happened yet.

Should ordained ministers preach and teach on this topic—about dividing the church, or reconciling the warring parties within the church?

In the history of American Methodism, there has been one moral issue that led to schism. Racism, manifest in the institution of slavery when it was legal and in segregation when it was legal, has led to multiple fractures in the Methodist connection through the centuries. In 1796, Richard Allen and others left a Methodist Episcopal church in Philadelphia, Pennsylvania, when they were told to vacate their places of prayer and make room for the white folks. They left, vowing never to return. From that episode, the African Methodist Episcopal Church was formed. Similar circumstances led to the formation of the African Methodist Episcopal Zion Church a short time later. The biggest separation of all happened in 1844, when slavery became an issue that American Methodism could no longer ignore, and the resulting division split the largest body of Methodist people into northern and southern churches. The reunion of those two groups eventually happened, but it took nearly a century. During the intervening decades, patterns of racial segregation became the norm in the church. Southern Methodism separated its black members into the Colored Methodist Episcopal Church. Northern and Southern Methodism both developed their systems of racially segregated congregations and conferences. When reunion came in 1939, a new organizational unit called the jurisdictional conference institutionalized racism as a matter of constitutional Methodism and ecclesiastical law with the creation of the Central Jurisdiction.

From the current disputes and the historic divisions within American Methodism, one could conclude that the truly difficult debates for the church are matters of social policy and political discussion. To be sure, they have been intense and important. From time to time, persons in the ordained ministry had to choose whether to teach and preach about such things.

In the meantime, along the way, the biggest and longest debates have centered on the ordained ministry itself.

Conflicts Focused on Ordination Itself

As powerful and as enduring as disputes on social issues have been, they are dwarfed in time and extent by the conflicts that Methodism has had over ordained ministry. Before Methodists were fighting over homosexuality, women's rights, health care, alcohol, or racism, we were fighting about ordained ministry. When Methodism was a fledgling movement within the Church of England, the Wesley brothers who founded the movement argued over ordination. When Methodism spread to the American colonies in the middle of the eighteenth century, there was a debate over how to meet the needs of Methodist people without an ordained ministry. When John Wesley (after the death of his brother Charles and after the conclusion of the colonies' successful war for independence) approved the ordination of Methodists in America, Francis Asbury balked at using Wesley's authorization as the basis for his ordination and insisted that the preachers endorse it.

Ordained ministry has been a key issue in every one of the major fights that has been waged within American Methodism. In the 1760s, when an unordained Maryland preacher named Robert Strawbridge took upon himself authority to administer the sacraments despite the express opposition from Mr. Wesley about performing such activities without ecclesiastical authorization, the place of an ordained ministry became a leading subject of debate in colonial Methodism. When the schism separating north and south occurred in 1844, it was not only about slavery but also about ordained ministry. One question was whether bishops could acquire or own slaves. Another question was whether anyone besides other bishops could exercise the discipline to prevent them from doing so. One of the costs of the reunification of Northern and Southern Methodism in 1939 was an agreement to the principle that the authority of the ordained ministry was subordinate to the role of race—black clergy, including black bishops, would be sequestered in the central jurisdiction to make sure that they had no ministerial place (and certainly no supervisory place) among white Methodists.

Meanwhile, throughout the nineteenth century and most of the twentieth, debates about the ordained ministry concerned the barriers to women in church leadership.

It was not until 1956 that The Methodist Church finally removed the last institutional barriers to full clergy rights for women.

Exemplar Practice Linked to Ordained Ministry

The ordained ministry became the exemplar of proper Methodist life and practice as well as the battleground for deciding what Methodist life and practice should properly be. Methodists decided to legislate their views on major social issues by linking them with the ordained ministry and turning them into matters of church law. Two divisive issues demonstrate this point succinctly.

The temperance movement within Methodism manifested itself in a peculiar way with respect to the ordained ministry. Church law in the twentieth century specified that laypeople who held office in local churches of Methodism were to abstain from the use of tobacco and alcohol. Church law also required that persons entering the ordained ministry had to sign statements that they would abstain from the use of tobacco and alcohol. Officially that church mandate remained in place until 1968. Church practices, however, were applied very differently. The provision concerning behavior of laity seems never to have been enforced, although it is certainly possible that local churches—through their quarterly conferences or church conferences—chose to apply it in their elections of leaders. It clearly was applied to the ordained ministry, however. Generations of Methodists approaching their ordinations had to sign documents committing themselves to abstinence from the use of tobacco and alcohol. There were exceptions in implementing this law. Candidates for ordination in tobacco-producing states such as North Carolina, Kentucky, and Virginia were advised that, though it was essential to commit to abstinence with regard to alcohol, the church could be flexible on the use of tobacco. It was a pragmatic approach to the application of church law in places where the offering plates might be quite empty if tobacco revenues were unwelcome.

The key point is that the ordained ministry was identified as the exemplar of discipline for the church. Enforced abstinence from beverage alcohol became a symbolic act of the church, mandated for the ordained ministry but viewed as exceptional or optional for the laity. Enforced abstinence from the use of tobacco became a regional option for those who were ordained.

In the closing decades of the twentieth century and well into the twenty-first, the same pattern has been chosen by The United Methodist Church with regard to homosexuality. While the aforementioned Social Principle on homosexuality is an action by the General Conference intended "to be instructive and persuasive" without being "considered church law" (*The Book of Discipline*, p. 97), there is an explicit set of church laws regarding homosexuality and the ordained ministry. "The practice of homosexuality is incompatible with Christian teaching. Therefore self-avowed practicing homosexuals are not to be certified as candidates, ordained as ministers, or appointed to serve in The United Methodist Church" (*The Book of Discipline*, ¶ 304.3, p. 206).

This is yet another example of the pattern of illustrative discipline that separates the ordained ministry from the rest of the church in United Methodism. It is peculiarly inconsistent to hold that the ordained ministry is a set of offices and orders within the church and then to insist on a major point of church law that separates the ordained ministry from the rest of the church. It also seems odd to apply as church law a rigid position that is different from the modestly ambiguous position in the Social Principles that instruct the church.

Historic Inconsistency

Such an inconsistency has occurred in the church before. Many branches of the broader Methodist family are woven into The United Methodist Church today. Among them are United Brethren, the Evangelical Association, the Methodist Protestant Church, the Methodist Episcopal Church, and the Methodist Episcopal Church, South. Within the separate histories that marked these bodies were differing points of view about the ordination of women. Some of these bodies objected theologically or practically to the roles of women in various forms of lay leadership, such as by denying women the opportunities to be global missionaries on behalf of the church. And attitudes differed among the branches of Methodism about whether laywomen could preach, whether they could be ordained, whether they could be elected as "laymen" among the delegates to General Conference. At different times in the history of American Methodism, women were licensed as lay preachers but were denied access to the ordained ministry. At other times, women were ordained as "local" deacons or "local" elders but were denied opportunities to be ordained as "traveling" elders.

This was not a matter of moral or spiritual character. It was a matter of using the ordained ministry as a separate category of people within the church. It was a means of using women as instruments to divide the church into different categories of people, presumably to mirror social practices in the prevailing culture rather than to exercise the ordained ministry as an office of the church.

Summary

From the emergence of Methodism in the middle of the eighteenth century until today, there have been on-going debates and disputes within the movement about the nature of the ordained ministry. And, along the way, ordained ministry has been turned into a partner of all other conflicts that affected the church. Sometimes, on issues of great social and political debate such as health care or immigration, the ordained ministry has been encouraged to keep silent. Sometimes, on issues of great debate such as temperance or homosexuality, the ordained ministry has been used as an exemplar of moral discipline that creates a separation from the rest of the church.

The consequences of all this have been to deprive the church of the resources of its ordained ministry at a time when they are needed most. So many of the debates and disputes about ordained ministry have been focused internally upon the rights granted by ordination, upon the exemplary behaviors that are expected after ordination, upon mechanisms that can be created to make sure that one has come close to perfection before ordination, and upon the ecclesiastical systems that can be in place to assure a comfortable career after ordination. Yet what the church needs is an ordained ministry that is empowered to look outward more than inward; to see the world as an arena for mission, not as an environment in which to seek comfort; to exercise not only the biblical mandate of pastor but also the biblical mandate of prophet; to transform what is evil in the world, not merely to condemn it; to tell the truth of the gospel and reconcile others to it.

The ordained ministry in The United Methodist Church has the opportunity to draw upon a heritage that has been linked with every great theological, social, personal, moral question that has been raised in recent centuries. The ordained ministry in The United Methodist Church has been identified to witness and work in the name of Jesus Christ for his mission in the world: in the face of evil, to confront it; in the encounter with theological error, to correct it; in the midst of injustice, to transform it; in the environment of ignorance, to overcome it; in the situations of despair, to create hope; in the circumstances of exclusion, to offer space at the Table; at the point of death, to proclaim resurrection.

For too long, the debates and disputes about ordained ministry in The United Methodist Church have been focused internally. It is time to look externally, outside the church, and find in the world the place of mission to which Jesus Christ sent his apostles. The ordained ministry is a continuation of that apostolic witness. It is not built upon professional techniques for finding comfort in the world. It is an empowered word offering transformation of the world.

Notes

1. The original designations were deacon, elder, and superintendent. But Francis Asbury quickly took to calling himself (and his fellow superintendent Thomas Coke) by the title *bishop*.
2. Richard P. Heitzenrater, *Wesley and the People Called Methodists* (Nashville: Abingdon, 1995), 34–35.
3. William B. Lawrence, "Has Our Theology of Ordained Ministry Changed?" in *Questions for the Twenty-First Century Church*, eds. Russell Richey, William Lawrence, and Dennis Campbell (Nashville: Abingdon, 1999), 157–58.
4. J. Bruce Behney and Paul H. Eller, *The History of the Evangelical United Brethren Church* (Nashville: Abingdon, 1979), 360.

CHAPTER 2

Pairing Grace and Law

Ordained ministry was a relative latecomer to the Methodist experience. For its first few decades, Methodism was a renewal movement within the Church of England. It functioned as a network or connection of groups under the general superintendency of John Wesley. Preachers delivered sermons at open-air gatherings, inside the walls of established churches, and in the confines of Methodist meeting houses. Some of these preachers were ordained, and others were not. Each served under the approving eye of Mr. Wesley with an authority that derived from his leadership of Methodism rather than their ordination (if, in fact, they were ordained).

There were many organizational units. Classes and bands met under the leadership of the laypeople who were trained and assigned to their responsibilities for small groups. Societies held large gatherings for praying and preaching and singing. Circuits with multiple preaching points were fashioned, and preachers were rotated through them by Mr. Wesley's appointment. He monitored his preachers, supplied them with published writings, and maintained the ministries of the movement (including the facilities in which they were housed) under his own direct, personal supervision.

As the decades passed, Wesley had to face the fact of his own mortality and his need for some plan of succession to manage the movement. In the 1760s, he devised a model deed and a pattern of trusteeship to care for real estate. In the later years, he came to the conclusion that the successor to his authoritative leadership would not be a person but a system.

For forty years prior to Wesley's formal approval of an ordained ministry within Methodism, there were gatherings of Methodist preachers to discuss matters of doctrine and discipline. Some of these preachers were already ordained in established ecclesiastical traditions. Others were lay preachers trained by the Wesley brothers and their movement to proclaim the gospel. All of them were present by invitation. They assembled in these meetings, called conferences.

But, as with so many things about Methodism, even the word *conference* had a special meaning. Beginning in 1744 with the very first conference, John Wesley said that the term applied not to the art of conversation or conferring but rather to the constituency of persons who assembled for the purpose of conferring. In other words, the term *confer-ence* referred not to the business that was discussed or to the agenda of items given attention, but to the community of persons who formed a body of members in covenant. There-fore, in a Methodist context, a conference is not an organiza-tional activity but an organic entity. It is a body, having members who are joined in covenant with one another. The conference became the governing authority of the church through preachers who were bound in covenant with one another.

This covenantal self-understanding was thus the foun-dation upon which Methodists established their ordained ministry. When John Wesley reached the practical conclusion that it would be necessary to have an independent Methodist body in the independent nation called the United States of America, he also had reached the theological conclusion that it was proper for Methodists to have their own ordained ministry. He dispatched Thomas Coke to ordain Francis Asbury, who accepted the mantle only after insisting that a conference of preachers affirm the determination that he be ordained.[1] Other ordinations followed. The practice was codified in Methodist law and eventually in a constitution. Within those strictures, the conference controlled the terms and the conditions that governed ordination.

Today in The United Methodist Church, the principle remains that ordained ministry is an expression of the conference. But that agency is distributed in various ways across a number of conferences: a person must be approved by his or her own "charge conference" before starting on the path toward certification for ordained ministry; laws governing the process to ordained ministry are enacted by the General Conference of the denomination; and those church laws are executed by the actions of each annual conference.

The term *annual conference* is another phrase that United Methodism uses in its own unique way. Just as the word *conference* implies a membership body rather than a meeting for the purpose of conferring, an annual conference is actually a membership body, not a yearly gathering of the members. It is the community in which ordained deacons and elders have their church membership—not in the local churches to which they may be appointed or with which they may be affiliated.

Together, this network or "connection" of conferences governs ordained ministry in The United Methodist Church. It is true that only bishops ordain persons, but no one gets to be an ordained minister in the denomination without the approval and affirmation of a succession of conferences—charge and annual—that bears the responsibility for implementing the legislative decisions of the General Conference. Hence, the authoritative successor to Mr. Wesley—for Methodism generally and for The United Methodist Church specifically—is the conference.

Of course, the debate endures and the institutional pattern continues to evolve regarding questions about who constitutes the conference. Actually, a connection of conferences shares in this authority. The General Conference of The United Methodist Church adopts legislation on all sorts of details concerning ordained ministry. The annual conferences, however, decide how those laws are to be applied.

It is clear, for example, that to be ordained deacon or elder an individual must hold the master of divinity degree (or its equivalent) from a theological school approved by an agency of the denomination or must have taken "basic graduate theological studies" including "courses" in specified fields such as Old Testament, New Testament, theology, church history, worship, evangelism, and church mission (*The Book of Discipline*, ¶ 324.4a, p. 224). There are some legislated controls to guide the decisions that have to be made about individual candidates and the courses they have taken. But ultimately each annual conference becomes the arbiter of whether those courses meet the criteria and conditions for ordination, and each annual conference becomes the sole judge of whether to include specific individuals within the ordained ministry of The United Methodist Church. Similarly the General Conference writes the laws that declare who may be excluded from the ordained ministry (*The Book of Discipline*, ¶ 304.3, ¶ 304.5, p. 206). But annual conferences decide how to apply those laws.[2]

Within the connection of conferences writing this legislation, applying these laws, and making these decisions, the persons who constitute each conference are proportionately sorted. General Conference, by the denomination's constitution, always has an equal number of clergy and lay delegates. Charge conferences, where the initial decisions are made to affirm individuals seeking to become candidates for ordained ministry, are overwhelmingly composed of laity. And the annual conference clergy session, where the final votes take place to determine whether an individual will be ordained, is still overwhelmingly a body of ordained ministers, though the designation of constituents who are eligible to vote on matters pertaining to ordained ministry is itself evolving. Once restricted to the clergy members in full connection, that franchise is now expanded to include the laypeople who are members of the annual conference board of ordained ministry (*The Book of Discipline*, ¶ 602.6, p. 369).

Notwithstanding these changing details, the fundamental principle remains. Conferences decide who will be ordained. Persons are received into conference membership before being ordained, and one must be a full member of an annual conference before ordination as a deacon or elder. All of this is defined by church laws and procedures.

Yet many people find this legislated and regulated process to be onerous. Some even find it downright repulsive — at least in the sense that the church appears to have so many legislative and regulatory hurdles in the path to ordination that it may repel some candidates for ordained ministry from enduring the process and pursuing the goal. It conveys the impression to many that this is a church built more upon law than upon grace. Indeed, one committee assigned to energize and revitalize the church asserted in the spring of 2010 that the denomination should be constructed with more freedom and grace, and with fewer rules.[3]

However, Methodism has from its beginning been characterized as a body that articulates and practices the Christian faith according to a method, and Methodism has for almost all of its history described its method in a *Discipline*. This is not an arbitrary term. Neither is it a legislative concept. It is rooted in a theological debate that is as old as Christianity itself and that was reargued during the Protestant Reformation of the sixteenth century.

One can read in the New Testament that salvation is entirely the work of God's grace through faith. Paul's letters to the Romans and Galatians, the decision of the apostolic council at Jerusalem reported in Acts 15, and the history of God's faithful people recounted in Hebrews 11 are just a few examples of scriptural authority for insisting that salvation is by grace alone. Paul wrote in Romans 1:17, where he drew upon the Old Testament prophet Habakkuk (2:4), that "the righteous live by faith."

At the same time, one can read in the New Testament that the Christian way of life is also defined as a life of discipleship, following Jesus in a disciplined way. His parables are routinely linked to exhortations about living according to certain standards. "Go and do likewise," Jesus advised those who heard about the practical care exercised by the Good Samaritan (Luke 10:37). "Love your enemies," Jesus instructed those who heard the Sermon on the Mount (Matt. 5:44). In the writings of the apostle Paul, there are numerous instructions about the proper way to live the Christian life, including his answers in 1 Corinthians (4:14–11:22) to a long list of questions submitted by a struggling church. And in the letter of James, the biblical message is unambiguous that "faith by itself, if it has no works, is dead" (2:17).

It appears that the scriptural message pairs two principles. On the one hand, salvation is available not by law but only by grace, which comes through faith. On the other hand, faith is present with saving power only where it is practiced according to Christian discipline.

During the theological debates among Protestant Reformers of the sixteenth century, the most eminent leaders of the Reformation disagreed on the way to link the paired principles of law and grace. For Martin Luther, the law had only two purposes: one was its civil use, namely to maintain civic and social order; the other was its confessional use, to make believers aware of their sins and their need for repentance. For John Calvin, the law had a third purpose. In addition to its civic and confessional uses, the "third use of the Law"[4] for Calvin was to provide a positive construction of the Christian life through which grace could actively work in redeeming the world.

Those who know the story of John Wesley's spiritual journey recall the importance of his religious experience on

May 24, 1738, while he was attending a meeting on Aldersgate Street in London. As he heard someone read from Martin Luther's "Preface to the Epistle to the Romans," Wesley wrote in his *Journal*, he felt his heart "strangely warmed" and received the assurance by grace through faith that he did trust in Christ alone for salvation. Yet if Luther's words provided an important element in Wesley's sense of assurance, Calvin's teachings played an even greater role in influencing Wesley's theological understanding. This is certainly true in understanding the "uses of the law." The approach or method in the Wesleyan theological motif affirms the principle in Calvin's interpretation of the Bible that there is a third use of the law, that structures of discipline offer positive methods for bringing faith to life, and that systems of church law are actually means for making grace available within the community of faith.

Properly understood, then, the disciplines of faith are actually a way to pair grace and law. This does not mean that every law of the church is an instrument of grace: some are merely bureaucratic annoyances; others are arrogant intrusions by people with enough power to impose them; still others (e.g., the laws of the church that embodied a doctrinal approval for slavery) are contrary to the gospel. But it does mean that the disciplines of faith offer the justifying and sanctifying grace of God to people and to the systems of the world not capable of finding their way to God's redeeming love through their own devices or in their own freedom of exploration.

Within Methodism, this theological conviction applies broadly to many aspects of faith and life. It unquestionably applies to understanding the ordained ministry. Every woman or man who is received into full clergy membership in The United Methodist Church must respond to a set of historic questions before being ordained. The questions address matters of both belief and behavior. They range from those that are rudely intrusive ("Are you in debt so as to embarrass your work in the ministry?") to those that are seemingly dated ("Will you visit from house to house?") to those that are theologically challenging ("Are you going on to perfection? Do you expect to be made perfect in love in this life?") (*The Book of Discipline*, ¶ 330, p. 5D).

The importance of these historic questions merits a separate discussion. However, their very existence is theologically significant, and the mandate of the church that every full member who is about to be ordained must answer them is theologically instructive. To enter the ordained ministry is to be entrusted by the church with responsibility for acts of teaching, preaching, visiting, conferring, presiding, serving, administering, and ordering that are more than the activities of a professional manager. They mediate the means of grace to people and to the world. And the authorization to determine who will be empowered—as ordained ministers—to be such agents of grace is viewed by Methodism as an authorization that can be granted only by the connection of conferences. The General Conference writes the laws that define this authority. The charge conferences approve persons who may feel called to embrace this authority. The annual conferences select the persons who are judged to have the gifts and the grace that allow them to be trusted with this authority.

Through this system of laws, the ordained ministry in Methodism expresses the church's covenantal life within "conference."

It is important not to underestimate the significance *Reduction* of this perspective. One can always reduce pastoral ministry to a set of professional tasks—delivering sermons, counseling people who are in trouble, managing volunteers, planning retreats, leading prayers, presiding at funerals, conducting weddings, raising funds, and posting blogs. One can even designate ordination as the authorization to engage in those tasks on behalf of the church. There is no doubt that such activities are useful in caring for individuals' needs, in constructing successful organizations, and in carrying out socially important functions. But defining ordained ministry in terms of these mechanisms involves a kind of reductionism that is incompatible with—and an incomplete form of—United Methodism; it limits the ordained ministry to human actions. What's missing is the mystery of God's grace empowering the church's ministries.

In Wesleyan theological language, there are many means of grace. Receiving the sacraments, studying Scripture, participating in prayer, and engaging in Christian conference are just a few of them. In Methodism, the ordained ministry has deep responsibility for offering various means of grace.

Yet the ordained ministry as an expression of Christian conferencing is itself an instrument of God's grace. That is, at least in part, what the apostle Paul meant in 1 Corinthians 4 where he invited his readers to think of the ministers in their midst, even the ones whose leadership seems to have become an excuse to sow seeds of division within the church, as "stewards of God's mysteries" (v. 1). The ordained ministry, therefore, is an expression of Christian conference when it embodies Jesus' mandate to love one's enemies. Ordained women and men in The United Methodist Church do not and will not agree on every point of doctrine or discipline. But ordained ministers have committed themselves to practicing the faith, which is dead unless it is embodied in works. Ordained ministers embrace the grace of reconciliation for others who are their adversaries within the covenantal community. To put the matter in its most basic terms, the ordained ministry within the conference provides the grace for debate that does not need to be destructive. The ordained ministry is a device to help the church experience grace in a way that surpasses political maneuvering.

Understood this way, the ordained ministry has the capacity to bear witness to the church that Christian conferencing is a means of grace. For that grace to be experienced, however, the church and its ordained ministry will have to create opportunities that have been vigorously resisted since the formation of United Methodism in 1968. Camps have formed around deep dedication to particular interpretations of the gospel. Caucuses have formed around careful commitments to identity politics. Campaigns have been built around notions that if we can just get the church organized correctly, we will generate enthusiastic support for programs that will renew the institution. Such mechanistic approaches to church life overlook the mystery of grace that is available in Christian conferencing and expressed in the church's ordained ministry.

Successful politicking in the church requires organizing one's friends. Stewardship of the mysteries of God involves loving one's enemies.

When the first conference of Methodist preachers assembled in 1744, three questions were posed for their deliberation: What to teach? How to teach? What to do? In a sense, the successive conferences within Methodism ever since that time have been struggling with those same three questions. They press the church and its ordained ministry to pursue with the greatest possible clarity the content of the faith, the means for communicating that content, and the practices of life that exhibit both the means and the meaning of Christian faithfulness.

The form of question/answer is not terribly evident in most annual conference gatherings nowadays. It is, however, the way that the clergy session of the annual conference — where all of the decisions about ordained ministry reside — continues to be conducted and recorded. Some of the questions are procedural, such as, where is the conference meeting? Others apply to the critical decisions about ordination, including, who [among us] are ordained elders? and, who are ordained deacons? Still others address changes in the relationships among the ordained ministers, such as, who are retired? and, who have withdrawn from the ordained ministry under complaints and charges? and, who have died?

But one of the first questions to be asked is an inquiry that goes straight to the heart and soul of the covenantal community: "Are all the ministers blameless in their life and official administration?" It is a question that must be answered by the members of the clergy session themselves. Various devices have been created to enable greater efficiency in answering or to avoid awkwardness when some ordained ministers have been publicly (or privately) accused of blamable conduct and are in the midst of having those complaints adjudicated. But the question is actually a matter of the discipline that determines who, among the covenantal community of the ordained ministers, remain worthy of being entrusted with the authorization of the church to convey the means of grace.

It is tempting to limit the reach of this question to matters of personal holiness that range from peccadilloes to major moral failures in areas such as financial or sexual misconduct. But the pairing of law and grace in the Wesleyan theological tradition as it applies to the blamelessness of persons in the ordained ministry should be viewed in a wider scope. For there is another kind of pairing that has to be used to measure relative holiness, namely the combination of personal and social holiness.

The grace that is manifest in works and the discipline that constructs a way of life according to the third use of the law are not merely matters of private moral conduct. They are also matters of social witness and systemic transformation. An ordained minister whose private moral conduct is above reproach but whose preaching has uttered nary a word about systems that deny health care to children is far from blame-less in her or his official roles. It is a means of grace (1) for the church to take seriously the discipline that embodies the theological commitments in Methodism and (2) for the ordained ministers to hold one another accountable to this way of life. It may be necessary to argue, within the covenant community, which systems oppress and which ones liberate. But if the ordained ministers in a conference are to receive the grace they are called to convey to one another, these debates should occur. Through them, ordained ministers can demonstrate to the whole church that it really is possible to identify both who one's enemies are and how to love them.

Notes

1. Historians debate the nature and legitimacy of this "conference" at Christmastime in 1784. But it launched the practice that has become normative for Methodism.
2. This is a clear provision in the constitution of the denomination. See *The Book of Discipline*, ¶ 33.

3. Richard Peck, "Call to Action Seeks to Increase Church Vitality," *Newscope* 38, no. 16 (April 21, 2010).

4. John Calvin, *Institutes of the Christian Religion*, 2.7.12.

CHAPTER 3

Discerning a Call to
Ordained Ministry

One of the many contributions that the Protestant Reformation made to Christianity was its assertion that any form of work can legitimately be described as a vocation. Whether one is a farmer or a physician, a nuclear physicist or a nurse practitioner, a computer engineer or a cook, work itself has potential value for enhancing human life and the social order. Mary's husband, Joseph, was a carpenter. The twin sons of Rebekah and Isaac, Jacob and Esau, were in farming and hunting. Ruth was a gleaner in the fields. Esther was a queen in a palace. Lydia sold purple dyes to prepare cloth. Paul made tents. The combination of skills, inclinations, aptitudes, and opportunities that one possesses can blend with the needs of people in the world into a career that can feel like a calling.

In some Christian communities, the term *vocation* is narrowly applied to the religious life. Certainly there are settings where vocation involves a deeper commitment than might be implied by a reference to a career choice. Anyone who enters a religious order or a monastic community that requires taking vows of celibacy and poverty is doing more than taking a job. That person is embarking upon a vocational journey that involves multiple forms of self-sacrifice. But a call to ordained ministry in The United Methodist Church does not immediately demand those sorts of deprivations. Celibacy is expected, but only in singleness, according to church law. The average annual compensation for ordained ministers in the denomination will not rival the averages for other highly educated professionals such as those practicing law and medicine. But a typical package of salary plus benefits for an ordained minister who is serving full-time will equal or surpass the levels of support earned by teachers, police officers, and others at midlevels of public service. In more than a few ministry settings, both as senior pastors of large-membership churches and in various kinds of specialized ministries, the compensation can be quite sizable.

The Ministry

So a call to ordained ministry does not necessarily mean a commitment to low wages or a tolerance for substandard working conditions. Nor does a call to ordained ministry necessarily mean a willingness to forgo the intimacy of marital and family relationships. At the same time, a call to the ordained ministry does require an openness to yield at least part of the control over one's life and career to the roles that sacred mystery and supervisory structures will have in one's activities. And a call to the ordained ministry does require a tolerance for being drawn into the circumstances that mark both the centers and the boundaries of human life. Everyone who enters the ordained ministry will at some time be called upon:

- to celebrate marriages and to deal with divorces;
- to be with a family as it brings an infant into the household and to be with a family as it buries a dead infant in the ground;
- to visit with people as they move into a new home and to visit with people as they find themselves newly homeless;
- to pray for those who are dying that they might be restored to life and to pray for those who are dying that they might peacefully die so they can be raised to new life;
- to counsel with persons who want to be reconciled with those from whom they have become estranged and to counsel with persons who want to take their own lives and end the wreckage of their wretched existence;
- to form coalitions with people of other faiths so that interfaith efforts can address neighborhood problems and to find that chasms of mistrust divide

religious communities that cannot discover any common ground;
- to preach sermons that thousands (in the pews or by recorded media) will hear and to preach sermons that no one will hear (because the prophetic edge of the message was unwelcome by those who were present);
- to deliver the bread and the cup from the Lord's Table to people who hope it will help bring change to their lives and to people who are quite adept at resisting the grace of change in their lives;
- to be energized by the Spirit who dwells in the church and to be enervated by the political strife that dwells in the church;
- to pray for people who labor for peace and to pray for people who are sent into war;
- to sit on boards with a mission to make a difference and to sit, bored, with the fear that great efforts are making no difference;
- to sit in a courtroom with someone who has been victimized by a grievous act and hope for justice;
- to sit in a prison with someone who has been the perpetrator of a grievous act and hope for mercy;
- to believe and to help everyone (including oneself) who may be struggling at the boundaries of unbelief.

Everyone who enters ordained ministry will be granted opportunities to enter into the most personal and most mysterious depths of human life. There are other professions, such as the practice of law, that pursue justice. There are other professions, such as the practice of medicine, that provide healing. There are other professions, such as teachers and counselors and construction engineers, that instruct or encourage or build. There are other professions, such as music and painting and poetry, that engage in great art. But there is nothing quite like the ordained ministry, if one feels called to it, that can in the span of a few short days create opportunities to celebrate a marriage as two people begin their life together, to construct low-income housing through a coalition of groups solving a serious problem together, to teach a group of preteen confirmands about the two thousand years of history that they are preparing to join, to teach a group of senior citizens the importance of making room for the ideas of these preteen confirmands who are on the verge of becoming their full-fledged brothers and sisters in Christ, to eulogize one of the old saints of the church at a memorial service, to baptize one of the new saints of the church in morning worship, and to proclaim in a sermon that each of these acts—while human in form and appearance—is the holy activity of God in the world.

That is what the ordained ministry is. But what does it mean to be "called" to ordained ministry?

The Call

It has been commonplace for ordained ministers to discuss their "calls" to ministry in personal or subjective terms. The first-person singular pronouns are used in describing my call to ministry or the occasion when I received the call. Those experiences tend to fall into two categories. One emerges from the sense of a continuing spiritual journey, being nurtured within the life of the church, culminating in an awareness and acceptance of beckoning from God that will lead to the act of ordination. The other emerges from a transformative moment or series of dramatic experiences that combine in a feeling that life is taking a totally new direction both personally and professionally. Both scenarios are legitimate and real. Anyone who characterizes a sense of call in either subjective way will find many others in ordained ministry who had similar experiences.

There is a long history of understanding ordained ministry as a vocation that completes and fulfills a spiritual life. Frances Willard, one of the great leaders among Methodists in the nineteenth century, described her experiences in Evanston, Illinois, as living in a Methodist hive. Her community was a colony of faith in the world, with the church and a network of allied institutions nurturing every aspect of life. That she was not ordained, or perhaps never felt called to be ordained, was a consequence of the bias in that nurturing community against women entering the ordained ministry. Nevertheless, during her era in the nineteenth century and through most of the twentieth century, there were systems that helped guide individuals toward accepting a sense of call. Camp meetings provided both a spiritual retreat and a social network. Sunday schools offered disciplined studies and practices for prayer. Programs for young people, such as the Epworth League, brought together music, recreation, spiritual formation, and social interaction. It was possible for a young Methodist who was baptized as an infant to attend Sunday school starting at the earliest age with the nursery class, to enroll in a program of study leading to confirmation as a member of the church, to participate in youth fellowship activities that offered opportunities to lead in public worship and prayer, to spend portions of each summer at a church camping program where vocational opportunities were as much of the scheduled routine as swimming or hiking, to matriculate at a church-related college for undergraduate study, to be invited to preach or speak in church on recognition days for students, to be encouraged by a pastor in the direction of ordained ministry, to go from college to seminary, and to seek approval from the church authorities for ordination.

Those were the elements of my story. And I shared it with many others in Methodist life across the years. But the notion of the nurturing process where a community of faith enables a person to experience a call to ministry is scarcely a Methodist invention. In the pages of the New Testament, Timothy was reminded of the faith that sustained his family, first in Lois his grandmother, then in Eunice his mother, and then in him (2 Tim. 1:5). Among the ancient church leaders, Cyprian famously said that one cannot have God for a Father who does not have the church for a Mother. If his language sounds sexist to North Americans in the twenty-first century, it was spiritually decisive for North African Christians in third-century Carthage. That sense of nurturing people toward a vocation or call to ordained ministry endured throughout the ages. It even revived in nineteenth-century America as a principle of the Mercersburg movement, one of whose leaders (a lay farmer named John Williamson Nevin) considered it an antidote to the excessive emotionalism of the so-called evangelical revival in his era.

The nurtured journey is one spiritual category of the subjective or inward call to ordained ministry.

The other is often a more dramatic experience. Individuals identify, rather than a sustained process, a specific—perhaps even spectacular—moment of awareness that a change of life is occurring. A new vocation is emerging. A powerful, indeed virtually irresistible, feeling of being called claims one's emotions. This can occur in many ways, as the following true but disguised cases will illustrate.

A man had enjoyed a successful career as an executive with a corporation ranked in the top 100 American companies. He was returning from an interview with another major business organization, where he had been offered an opportunity to become its chief executive officer. Not only would the new position be personally fulfilling and financially lucrative: it would be the capstone of a great career. But by the time he returned home from the interview, he had decided not only to turn down the job but to leave corporate life altogether and enroll in theological school, where he could prepare for ordained ministry.

A woman who had reached middle age was living comfortably, active in her career, married to a successful professional man, and sharing with him the responsibilities for their nearly adult children. In circumstances that she did not initially recognize, their marriage was experiencing strains. To her great surprise, her husband filed for divorce. In the months and years that followed, she discovered that multiple forms of healing helped her endure and that much of her well-being was mediated to her through the ministries of the church. Within this dramatic set of changes, she felt a strong emotional call to pursue the ordained ministry as a way to complete the healing of her own soul and as a way to bring saving grace to others.

A man who was little more than a decade away from normal retirement age sat in a class at a theological school and told the story of his vocation. As a college student, he had felt called to ordained ministry. But pressures from his family to find a more lucrative career while still being of service to others led him to law school. He achieved much and earned a lot more in his decades as an attorney. Then, in his fifties, he heard the call again. He said it was the same sense of call that he had rejected so many years earlier. He resigned from his law firm, enrolled in seminary, and reclaimed the vocation he had abandoned long ago, knowing that his time in ordained ministry might be rather brief but it would finally be an embrace of the Holy Spirit whom he had pushed aside.

A young woman had gone through her high school years and college experience in what she described as a self-indulgent and hedonistic style of life. Religion had never been part of her journey. But a chance encounter with a spiritually motivated acquaintance began a series of steps that led her to embrace the Christian faith. Not long after, her religious awakening burgeoned into a vocational aware-ness. She felt deeply that God was calling her not simply to the Christian life, but to the ordained ministry of the Christian church.

Within this subjective category of "call" to ordained ministry, there are many variations and nuances. Whether it is a steadily evolving feeling nurtured by the community of faith or a dramatically transforming experience that is iden-tified as a specific moment of decision, the inward sense of being called is an important aspect of vocation.

But in the Christian church generally and in United Methodism particularly, it is not the only one. Simply because one feels called does not necessarily mean one is called. The ordained ministry belongs to the church. So the church has a decisive role in discernment about vocation. A call is not a self-authenticating experience. A call to the ordained ministry is both inward and outward. One can legitimately claim that one has a vocation to the ordained ministry only if one asserts it as an individual and if the church asserts it about that individual.

Occasionally there are people who fervently insist that they have deeply felt, directly received, and devoutly embraced a call from God to the ordained ministry. Sometimes, with great emotion, they express astonishment that the church would put impediments in their way to delay or prevent their personal fulfillment of this vocation. Occasionally, but far more rarely in the present age, an individual is approached by church leaders and encouraged to pursue ordained ministry because they have perceived in this person a set of gifts and a presence of grace. Someone might even say to such a person, "God is leading you to this."

The Vocation

Yet unless both the inward and outward dimensions of call are present, it is not vocation. Some deep, subjective feeling is not tantamount to a call. Some clear, objective observation is not tantamount to a call. A call to ordained ministry is present when both the inward and the outward dimensions of it are present and affirmed, by the person and by the church.

In the twenty-first century, United Methodism has to give renewed and revitalized attention to both of those dimensions. The whole experience of a nurturing system that can lead toward a call has eroded to the point of ineffectiveness. Of all the aspects of church programming that can be measured statistically, the one that has most steeply declined is Sunday school attendance. As a program of Christian education, it cannot be counted upon in its present form to fulfill the nurturing needs of the church's mission. A viable alternative is needed, but none is in place or at hand. Some other elements of the nurturing system are still present. But most—church camping programs, church-related colleges, and ministries on college campuses, for example—have seen their revenues from the church eroded if not eliminated entirely. Meanwhile, United Methodism has paid only marginal attention to the means of confronting people, especially young people, with opportunities for dramatically transformative experiences that effect emotionally constructive decisions. Plenty of subjective energy has been expended within the church on rage at terrible social injustices, on animosity toward adversaries, on homosexuality or abortion, and on outrage at various approaches to biblical interpretation. Far less energy has been devoted to understanding and allowing constructive, emotional commitments to liberation from addictions, violence, hatred, bigotry, self-indulgence, greed, and other forms of captivity. Bringing people to emotionally constructive decisions about pursuing the ordained ministry is an increasingly lost practice in the church. United Methodism in the twenty-first century must turn its heart and soul and mind and strength to reviving the methods for evoking the inward dimension of vocation.

At the same time, the outward dimension of call must be revived and revised if The United Methodist Church is to have an effective ordained ministry in the twenty-first century. Among the complications is the fact that there is no one theology of ordained ministry upon which the church relies when implementing its outward dimensions of call. There are multiple theologies that have fed like tributary streams into Methodism's understanding of ordination. It is historically untenable and theologically unsustainable to argue for a singular approach to ordained ministry. What the church has done is accumulate its numerous perspectives and retain them all. As historian Russell Richey has noted, theological preparation for ordained ministry is a good illustration of this approach. American Methodism went from an individualized mentoring or tutoring method to a designated reading method to a course of study method to a method that mandated or expected theological education at the master's-degree level. But in so doing, the church never jettisoned or set aside the previous methods. All of them still remain in place with some measure of affirmation or requirement.

One practical consequence of this is that the denomination seeks discernment about the outward dimension of the call by appearing to put individuals through immensely complex and unnecessarily time-consuming processes to reach the moment of ordination. From an initial conversation, between a person who feels inwardly called and the local pastor, to the climactic outward act as the hands of a bishop are laid upon the head of an ordinand, will require at least five years but may consume ten years or longer. During that time, the individual who has felt the inward dimension of a call must have affirmative votes from two local church bodies, one district committee on ordained ministry, and the clergy session of an annual conference where two votes (at least two years, but possibly as many as eight years, apart) discern that the dimension of an outward call is sustained. Moreover, most of those affirmative votes have to be renewed annually. Through this process, the individual will have been examined psychologically and physically, will have had a criminal background check, and will have completed some theological education; its path can either be straight through baccalaureate and master's degrees or indirectly through various maneuvers that the church has chosen to judge as equivalent.

Notwithstanding the theologically essential requirement that a call have both inward and outward dimensions and the ecclesiastically practical requirement that the church put in place appropriate methods for outwardly discerning a call, this system is regrettably complex and functionally unsuitable.

Discerning a call to ordained ministry is both a personal and an ecclesiastical matter. It is also a process that involves both the mind and the soul. As Charles Wesley pleaded in the text of a hymn: "Unite the pair so long disjoined, knowledge and vital piety."[1] To engage in discernment of the inward and outward dimensions of call is to engage both the mind and the spirit.

One of the truly great novels in American literary history is *The Damnation of Theron Ware*, or *The Illumination*.

In Harold Frederic's tale, Theron Ware is a Methodist preacher from the central part of New York State who apparently has significant gifts for pulpit oratory but whose intellectual and spiritual formation for ordained ministry are both sorely lacking. He imagines himself appointed to a large and prominent church, but upon hearing that he has been appointed to a small and inferior one, he lacks the spiritual resources and disciplines to conduct an effective ministry or to avoid scandalous behavior. He imagines himself writing a book, but he lacks the resources and disciplines of mind to choose a topic, engage in the research, or focus on the act of composing a text.

Real preachers in Methodism, rather than fictional ones, have rarely been found to lack both the mind and the spirit for ministry. But, at various times, some efforts at inward and outward discernment have given excessively imbalanced attention to one or the other.

In the middle of the nineteenth century, for example, Methodist laity began to voice concerns that preachers might have been spiritually dedicated to the ordained ministry but were intellectually lacking in preparation for the calling. People in the pews were in some cases better educated than their preachers. People in the pews were pondering deeper and more difficult questions than their preachers were willing or able to address. Out of that experience came a decision by Methodist laity to begin urging better education for clergy and strategic action to create theological schools connected to the church.

In the latter part of the twentieth century, laity echoed a concern that ordained ministers seemed deficient in their spiritual readiness to lead complex institutions with an informed vision. Theological schools began adjusting their curricula to require spiritual formation as part of their master's degree requirements for future clergy. And they began to search for ways, in graduation requirements or in continuing education programs, to equip the ordained ministers of the future with the spiritual qualities of servant leadership.

Through such initiatives, theological education in preparing women and men for faithful leadership in Christian ministry becomes an aspect of the discernment process. It is an aspect of the inward call, because it pushes the mind and the spirit of the individual to confront more deeply the nature of biblical texts, the history of the Christian movement, the ethical issues of the age, and the changing global as well as regional demographic contexts in which an ordained minister's work will unfold. It is an aspect of the outward call as well, because it pushes the church to grasp that ordained ministry is not about organizational maintenance but the transformation of social and personal life.

To be truly called is to be invited to embrace that mission.

Note

1. Charles Wesley, "Come, Father, Son, and Holy Ghost, to Whom We for Our Children Cry," *The United Methodist Hymnal* (Nashville: Methodist Publishing House, 1964), no. 3440.

CHAPTER 4

Discovering Places for Ordained Ministry

Like a number of terms in the Methodist lexicon, the word *call* has a meaning that differentiates it from some usages in other Christian bodies. For Methodism, it applies to (1) the concept of vocation in the broadest sense—a call to Christian life and practice for all baptized believers, lay and ordained; and (2) a call to the ordained ministry through offices that are situated within the life of the church and are exercised on behalf of the church for the sake of the church and the world. For Methodism, *call* does not apply to specific places where an ordained minister engages in the activities authorized by ordination.

Baptists, Lutherans, Presbyterians, and even Episcopalians speak of a "call" from a parish or congregation whereby persons who are—or who are about to be—ordained can become the ministerial leaders of those local settings. They are invited to accept either senior or subordinate positions on church staffs as employees hired by the community that calls them.

Independent or entrepreneurial church leaders, some of whom are ordained by various associations or congregations, speak about being called to launch new ministries, to help foster an emerging faith community, or to plant a new church in some neighborhood. They may use sacred language to articulate this as a call from God to begin a new ministry where none exists, in which case they are not called or hired by a community because the community is what they intend to create rather than enter. Or they may use secular language to articulate this as a market opportunity or a niche that no other religious group has recognized as a region with resources to tap and needs to meet. There is biblical warrant for such a sense of call in the report of a vision that Paul experienced, where a man called him to come to Macedonia. According to Acts 16:9–10, this was both a human and a divine call.

Sent as an Apostle

In The United Methodist Church, one is "called" to the ordained ministry but not to the place where one serves in ordained ministry. Rather, one is sent or appointed to a place of ministry. There is biblical warrant for this as well. A disciple is one who follows, and Jesus had a large following of them. An apostle is one who is sent, and Jesus—as the earthly teacher and as the risen Lord—did a lot of sending according to the New Testament. In anticipation of his suffering and death, he sent seventy on a mission as an advance team to the places that he would visit on his journey to Jerusalem (Luke 10:1–11). On the day of his resurrection, he sent the eleven disciples from a mountain in Galilee to "make disciples of all nations, baptizing them in the name of the Father and of the Son and of the Holy Spirit" (Matt. 28:19). He sent Mary Magdalene to tell the others that he was ascending to God (John 20:17–18). He sent Paul to preach his name "before Gentiles and kings and before the people of Israel" (Acts 9:15; see also Gal. 1:15–16).

United Methodism views the placement of ordained ministers in this vein. They are sent to regions or locations or charges. They are, in this sense, apostolic ministers; they are sent by the church to situate themselves in places, to travel circuits, to serve people, and to engage in the transformation of the world. They are not called by those people or those regions but rather are sent to those people and regions as agents of the mission of the church.

When John Wesley sent Francis Asbury to the American colonies as a lay preacher and later authorized him to be ordained and to superintend The Methodist Episcopal Church in the United States of America, Asbury was sent with a mission to reform the continent and to spread scriptural holiness over the land. Today in The United Methodist Church, that mission is framed as making disciples for the transformation of the world. In both expressions, the church's ordained ministry is sent into the world with a missionary mandate to reform, transform, and disciple.

One key difference between describing ordained ministers as called by congregations or parishes and as sent to places for ministry is that the site of the ministerial appointment is not an ecclesiastical institution but rather a social or geographical region. One is sent to a place, perhaps a neighborhood in a specific city, in which a local church may be available as the base of missionary operations for that region; one is not called simply to care for a congregation. One is sent as an apostle of the risen Lord for discipling and transforming that territory.

Yet some are sent as ordained elders and others are sent as ordained deacons.

Sent as Elders or Deacons

When the decisive action of the 1996 General Conference replaced the sequential orders of ministry with the separate, substantive orders of elder and deacon, a significant part of the act was to designate specific forms of ministry for which each order is authorized. As expressed in the laws of the denomination through its *Book of Discipline*, elders are ordained to engage in the ministries of "Word, Sacrament, Order, and Service." They are authorized to preach and teach the Word of God, to provide pastoral care, to administer the sacraments, and to order the church for its mission in the world (¶ 332, p. 240). According to that same *Book of Discipline*, deacons exercise their ministries through teaching and preaching the Word of God, through contributing leadership in worship, through assisting elders in administering the sacraments, and through a variety of pastoral acts: forming and nurturing disciples, celebrating marriages, conducting funerals, and manifesting the mission of the church in the world (¶ 328, pp. 230–31).

These legislative descriptions of the roles assigned to the two types of ordained ministry are expressed in the rituals for ordaining deacons and for ordaining elders. During services of ordination, each person being ordained to the office of elder is told by the presiding bishop to "take authority as an elder to preach the Word of God, to administer the Holy Sacraments, and to order the life of the Church," while each person being ordained deacon is told to "take authority as a deacon to proclaim the Word of God, and to lead God's people to serve the world."

In that process of conferring authority on persons who enter distinct and separate orders of ministry, The United Methodist Church established a structure of ordained ministry that was rather unusual. In some ways, it looked more like the orders of deacon and priest in the Roman Catholic Church (whose understanding of the priesthood is quite different, of course) than any of the predecessor bodies out of which United Methodism immediately developed. What had been a sequential ordering of ministry in most of mainstream Methodism and a single order of ministry in some of the predecessor church bodies all but disappeared. A new, twofold structure of ordination with separate offices having distinct authorizations has now appeared.

One could say that the changes in 1996 introduced relatively little alteration in the order of elder, other than its being no longer the second of two stages in an ordination process. However, the order of deacon is both a new and continually evolving form of ministry. It is in the process of being changed from time to time, on occasion by legislative enactment[1] and on occasion by ecclesiastical practice.[2]

There is a long history to the diaconate in Methodism. Besides the order of ministry that has been the first stage in the sequential ordination process, Methodism has had both the ministry of deaconesses (who still have a place in the structure of the church) and diaconal ministers (who are no longer being credentialed within the church). Both of those service ministries are understood as being for laity, not ordained ministers. For ordained deacons in United Methodism since 1996, however, a ministry as deacon is distinguished by its authorization to lead the church in matters of service. Deacons serve in fields such as education, health care, social work, community development, criminal justice, social justice, youth work, children's work, music, global outreach, and various other activities. Deacons are based in local churches, in denominationally connected institutions, and in community-based organizations. It is not simply that they serve. They are authorized, ordained, appointed, and sent to exercise the leadership of the church in their modes of serving.

Note important nuances in distinguishing facets of the ordained ministry exercised by deacons and elders when they are sent. Elders do not formally (or normally) find the places to which they are sent. Deacons do formally (and normatively) find the places where they will serve and then request that the bishop send them. Elders are consulted about the places to which the bishop intends to appoint them. Deacons consult with the bishop about the places to which they have been invited. But both elders and deacons are appointed and, hence, are sent in the pattern of apostolic ministry.

By the early twenty-first century, much of this under-standing had faded into the background of ordained ministry in The United Methodist Church. The trend toward lengthening the number of years that one served consecutively in the same appointment seemed to erode the notion of being sent to a place and instead acquired a sense of being settled in a parish. The methods used to measure and assess effectiveness in ministry tended to be based upon metrics that were internal to the institution or congregation: membership, worship attendance, pastoral salary, operating budget, and other organizational data.

As a mission movement, however, Methodism in the coming decades will need to find ways for assessing the effectiveness of ordained ministers by metrics that are appropriate to the actual appointment in the region. At its most basic level, this should mean that quantitative assess-ments include comparative assessments. In any period of three to five years, for example, it is vital to determine how worship attendance has changed when compared to the population changes in the region. Beyond this, at a more missional level, the quantitative assessments should include measurements of the transformation occurring in the region. Has the high school graduation rate improved? Has the number of persons living on the street declined? Has the percentage of parents attending school conferences with their children's teachers grown? For the church to be truly in the mission of making disciples and transforming the world, the ordained ministry has to allow its effectiveness to be measured by methods that calculate not only the impact on an institutional church but also on a needy world.

During a visit to Hong Kong in the winter of 2009, I had an opportunity to talk with some church leaders about their approaches to mission and ministry. One described the measurements that they use to determine whether a new church that was planned and planted has in fact become a church. They say that three things are needed to declare that a church exists in that place. One is the presence of an identifiable community that meets regularly for worship. The second is an educational program for the children in the neighborhood, such as after-school tutoring or remedial reading. The third is a civic improvement activity, such as a drug-abuse counseling center or a health clinic that cares confidentially for the victims of domestic violence. Only when all three elements are present is a church deemed successfully established in the region.

For ordained ministry in The United Methodist Church to have an effective future, it must reach into the resources of its past and rediscover the power of apostolic ministry not only for the sake of the church but for the sake of the world. Words like *appointment* and *assignment* are not merely managerial references to means for deploying preachers or designating bishops to move to spots on a map. They are missional and theological terms for connecting the existence of an ordained ministry with the purposes for which the church created it. The mission will be further enhanced if ordained ministers who are appointed to distinct local churches within the same city or community or school district understand their ministries—and have their ministerial effectiveness assessed—by the transformative impact that they have by working collaboratively, as a team, on matters that are common to the region. If a city council passes an ordinance that appears to foster discrimination against an ethnic, religious, national, or immigrant group, an individual ordained minister in an isolated congregation can feel powerless to oppose it. But if the ordained ministers who are appointed in different local churches or specialized ministries to that same region were to see a connectional opportunity to serve the needs of those persons victimized by discrimination, then the church really can be led by its ordained ministry to make disciples and transform the world.

Such things have happened, and in the not-too-distant past. In the 1960s, a group of white Methodist ministers in

Mississippi led the way toward desegregating the church and the state. Some lost the support of their parishioners. Some lost the opportunity to stay in their local appointments. But all of them found that the power of God's grace can still be active in making disciples and in transforming the world. Occasionally when ordained ministers are reluctant to risk their personal and professional security to engage in such prophetic witness, laity act in ways that remind their ordained servant leaders what it means to serve and to lead. So, for instance, in the first decade of the twenty-first century, when political disputes seemed to make it impossible for states and for citizens on the U.S.-Mexico border to address immigration issues in decent and humane ways, groups of laypeople—including many United Methodists—formed Samaritan ministries and went into the desert to provide water and food to immigrants.

To achieve more missional methods for assessing the effectiveness of ordained ministry, new things will have to be accomplished not only by those who are sent but also by those who do the sending.

The annual conferences decide who will be ordained.

The bishops decide where the ordained will be sent.

The Office and Role of Bishop

Within the structures of the ordained ministry in The United Methodist Church, the office of bishop is quite possibly the most unusual. John Wesley did not intend for the title to be used at all by The Methodist Episcopal Church in the United States of America. He considered himself to be the general superintendent of the Methodist movement, and he expected Thomas Coke and Francis Asbury to function under the title of superintendent for the American church. Within a few years of Asbury's ordination at Coke's hand in 1784, however, Coke and Asbury began to claim the title *bishop*. Wesley protested, but there was nothing he could do to change the situation. Besides, Wesley himself had come to terms with the idea of authorizing Methodist ordinations by understanding himself as an ordained priest leading this movement in a status equivalent to that of a bishop as the office is described in the New Testament epistles. Hence, as a "scriptural *episcopos*," he had the biblical standing to ordain (or to authorize ordinations) as a bishop would. Asbury and Coke claimed no more authority than that. They simply added the title to the office. Wesley had provided the theological framework for an understanding of *bishop*. Asbury, Coke, and those who came after them simply adopted the title.

For the ensuing decades in American Methodism, bishops were elected and ordained.

Not every tributary flowing into United Methodism today embraced the title. One of those tributaries, the Methodist Protestant Church, came into being through a vehement protest against the office. With the reunion of major Methodist bodies in 1939, that impasse was broken. The office of bishop remains as an important facet of the ordained ministry. Originally elected by the General

Conference, bishops are now elected in the United States by jurisdictional conferences and outside the United States by central conferences.

Today bishops are "consecrated," not ordained to their office. They do not belong to a different order of ministry, for they remain elders. But their church membership, upon election, moves from their annual conferences to the Council of Bishops, the only place in the life of the church where they have a right to vote. (And they lose that franchise when they retire.) The authorizations that they have as ordained ministers derive from their ordinations as elders, not from their consecrations as bishops; they preach the Word, they administer sacraments, they engage in ministries of service, and they order the life of the church. Their roles as bishops are administrative or, more properly speaking, presidential. They are general superintendents of the denomination. They oversee all of the spiritual and temporal affairs of the church. They preside at the sessions of the annual conferences to which they are assigned. They share the role of the presiding office with their colleagues in jurisdictional conferences. And they preside at sessions of the General Conference, if asked to do so by a committee on presiding officers. They preside at services of ordination. In that capacity as presider, they ordain. But they do not decide who gets to be ordained. They can speak in conferences only in the role as a presiding officer, never in the role of a participant, unless the conference votes to grant permission to do so. They appoint ordained ministers to their places for service, but they do not decide who is eligible to be appointed. They make sure, while presiding, that the clergy session of the annual conference votes on the character of all persons in ministry (without themselves having the right to vote on the determination of character). They preside over the processes that have to be followed when an ordained minister commits (or is accused of committing) an administrative or judicial offense against the law of the church. In their presidencies, they are the recognized leaders of the annual conferences to which they are assigned, but they are not members of their annual conferences, so they cannot serve on any of the committees created by the conference.

Bishops have immense power in the life of the church, and if they act deftly, they can exercise even more influence than they have power. They do not decide who gets to be ordained because only the clergy session of the annual conference can make that determination. Yet the clergy session of an annual conference can make those decisions only upon the recommendation of its board of ordained ministry, and nobody gets elected to that board without a nomination by the bishop. Nobody speaks during the conference session unless the bishop, as presiding officer, recognizes the person to speak. No motion or resolution appears on the agenda of the conference if the bishop rules it out of order. (Of course, most of these actions are matters of parliamentary procedure that can be appealed to the house, provided that the person seeking an appeal can be recognized by the presiding officer and granted permission to speak.) Finally, bishops send ordained ministers to the sites where they will serve. All appointments to places of ministry are made by the bishop. Such decisions cannot be arbitrary or idiosyncratic, for there are mandates about consultation with the persons affected before appointments are made. Even so, although consultation is required, compliance is expected. Concurrence with the appointment is not negotiated. In the end, an ordained minister is sent — and goes.

Despite this aggregation of power in the office of bishop, none of it is a consequence of ordination. All of it is the consequence of presidential position. And some of that is no longer what it once was. The original cohort of bishops, beginning with Asbury, itinerated throughout the connectional church and lived wherever they wished. Now they must live within a house provided by the annual conferences to which they are assigned, their presidential and appointive authorities are limited to the annual conferences where they are assigned,[3] and they cannot serve more than twelve consecutive years in any assignment.

Prior to 1980, bishops did not have a mandatory retirement age. But now they must retire in a year that is determined by their birth dates and by the denomination's quadrennial calendar. Prior to the formation of The United Methodist Church in 1968, consultation about pastoral appointments was not mandated or required. But now they adhere to a process that, following consultation, takes into consideration both the needs of persons to be appointed and the needs of places where appointees are sent. Prior to the reunion that formed The Methodist Church in 1939, bishops could determine that any legislation passed by the General Conference was in conflict with church law or with the church's constitution.[4] But with the formation of The Methodist Church and continuing into The United Methodist Church today, a Judicial Council was created by the Constitution to make determinations of legality or constitutionality and to review bishops' decisions of law in conference sessions.

While none of these items is an expression of ordained ministry, all of them have immense influence over the nature and function of the ordained ministry. As elders ordained to ministries of word, order, sacrament, and service, United Methodist bishops have collectively brought the power of the Word to bear on a wide array of global issues—peace, poverty, health, and education. As the officers of the church who are not only ordained to order but also assigned a supervisory responsibility for all the spiritual and temporal affairs of United Methodism, the bishops are uniquely positioned to hold the church accountable for its mission and management. They can celebrate the sacraments and engage in acts of service anywhere in the world. They can, as itinerant general superintendents of the church, model the mysteries of the sacraments when they baptize as a sign of God's grace and promise or when they preside at the Lord's Table offering the bread and the cup inclusively to all people who come by faith in Christ (as they individually confess it) without regard to age or church affiliation or any other impediment. They can serve, nobly and sacrificially, by delivering anti-malarial kits to protect children in Africa or by breaking down barriers to reconciliation at international borders.

In the twenty-first century, there are even more specific opportunities for bishops in their superintending of the ordained ministry. They alone are empowered to appoint. Therefore, they uniquely are positioned to define the methods of assessment that will be used to decide where the ordained ministers will be appointed. If the bishops choose to privilege such organizational and ecclesiastical criteria as worship attendance, budgets, and the number of new disciples who are recruited according to membership statistics, the mission of the church will narrow to concerns for institutional management. If the bishops choose to consider such world-transforming criteria as public health, childhood education, and deliverance from poverty, the mission of the church will expand to its full expression of making disciples for the transformation of the world.

Another opportunity for bishops to seize even more aggressively is to open the limits of appointment-making beyond the boundaries of the annual conferences or episcopal areas to which they are assigned. Only annual conferences decide who will receive ordination and who will remain in the ordained ministry. But bishops, as the itinerant general superintendents of the church, have

global freedom to appoint ordained ministers with grace
to places where their gifts can address needs. Bishops
can transfer ordained ministers from membership in
their own annual conferences to other annual conferences—
not arbitrarily, to be sure, but missionally. Technical
resources exist for bishops to become knowledgeable and
to have access to data about all of the ordained ministers
in the United Methodist connection. The concept of a
collective episcopacy embodies a principle that all
bishops are peers of one another. The Restrictive Rule,
which inhibits the church from altering its itinerant
general superintendency, empowers bishops to act and
think not narrowly about their own area assignments as
their priority (as if they were diocesan leaders in another
denomination or chief executive officers of an annual
conference corporation). Instead they can see the connec-
tionally global church as their priority.

Finally, bishops are ordained ministers as elders of the
church. But when they reach the mandatory retirement age,
a strange thing happens to them. They retain their church
membership within the Council of Bishops, but they can no
longer participate by voting on any decisions that
affect the life of the church. Only if they are restored to
active service and assigned to some area for emergency
purposes do they exercise their ordination to order. They
can still preach the Word (if they are invited somewhere, or
intrude themselves somewhere) or celebrate the sacraments wherever two or three are gathered. They can still

engage in service, like every layperson and ordained minister, in any capacity they choose. But, without having their ordination as elders taken away, they have the capacity to participate in ordering the life of the church taken away.

This is an anomaly that the church could resolve by making a decision about bishops who reach the point of retirement. They could return as elders to the clergy membership of the annual conferences from which they were elected. There they could continue to engage in the ministry of order, by voting in the clergy session on recommendations submitted by boards of ordained ministry and on the character of clergy members in the annual conference. They could speak in the business sessions of the conference. They could vote on electing clergy delegates to the General Conference and to jurisdictional conferences. They could even be elected delegates to those bodies if their clergy colleagues chose to do so. They could be called upon to preside at charge conferences, not as bishops but as elders. And they could, as clergy members of annual conferences who establish a charge conference affiliation the way all retired deacons and elders do, participate in helping the church identify, recruit, affirm, encourage, recommend, and guide candidates for the ordained ministry. There are many places for ordained ministers to fulfill their ordination. Even those who have retired, including the ones who have held the office of bishop, can enter those places.

Notes

1. *The Book of Discipline,* ¶ 328, p. 231, allows a bishop to "grant local sacramental authority to the deacon to administer the sacraments in the absence of an elder."
2. Some elders who serve as senior pastors of churches with deacons on the church staff have been known to allow deacons to preside at communion. Some bishops have been known to seek licenses as local pastors for ordained deacons so they could be appointed as pastors in charge of local churches.
3. A visiting bishop can, of course, be invited to preside (or to ordain) by the bishop assigned to an episcopal area. And bishops from outside of the episcopal area do preside at church trials in annual conferences.
4. The Methodist Episcopal Church, South, had created a judicial council in the years just before reunion. That new constitutional entity then became part of the reunited church.

CHAPTER 5

Signs and Symbols of Ordination

A few decades ago, a television commercial suggested there were three ways one could identify someone as a physician. He (and this was in the days when professional cohorts like medical doctors were likely to be gender specific) wears a white coat, carries a black bag, and drives a Buick. Nowadays, it is hard to imagine that any of those signs can be presumed. Although many physicians do wear lab coats in the clinic or the hospital, others wear scrubs or pullover shirts with casual pants. Few carry black bags, unless the bags happen to contain either mobile communication devices or laptop computers. And their means of transportation cannot be limited to any stereotype. The television character called simply House, a physician though scarcely a typical one, rides a motorcycle. Some demonstrate their commitment to fitness by riding their bicycles to the office. Others choose from an array of vehicles, including luxury cars and pickup trucks and super-small minis that operate primarily on electric power.

Dress, Address, and Duties?

When ordained ministers are depicted in contemporary media, they are most likely to be costumed in recognizably conventional attire. A clerical collar will denote a Roman Catholic or Episcopal priest. The long-running cable television series *Seventh Heaven* featured one of the central characters as a Protestant minister clad in a black academic gown for worship. In a popular BBC series, the vicar of Dibley dresses very casually when she is at home in the vicarage, but she typically dons what the Brits describe as a "dog collar" for church meetings and wears an alb with surplice for liturgies.

Popular media rarely handle religious matters well (although *The Vicar of Dibley* may be an exception). The behavior and appearance of ordained ministers tend to be stereotyped by producers and directors. They often demonstrate how little they know.

Certainly when it comes to attire, there is nothing that can be described as the typical dress for an ordained United Methodist. Moving from one worship space to another in the same denomination, an observer can be led by ordained United Methodists in various garbs. One has an alb with surplice or chasuble and stole in the color of the liturgical season. Another wears an alb tied with cincture over a clerical collar rabat. Still another is clad in an academic robe with a stole that blends with the interior décor of the worship space. Still another might lead worship in a pullover shirt or blouse that could be worn to the golf course if one has a tee time after the service. Other ordained ministers work in casual button-down shirts or blouses that may or may not be tucked in at the waist, or (if one happens to visit on a day when the children's vacation Bible school program is being celebrated) in a pair of shorts with a T-shirt and sandals.

Context, not convention, determines what the properly dressed ordained minister will wear. A casual, contemporary shirt goes nicely with a casually dressed congregation of persons who assemble for a so-called contemporary style of worship. An alb and stole signify that the context will not be the lifestyles of the worshipers but the long history of ecclesiastical liturgy. An academic gown or a business suit will convey a consciousness of economic class or social taste that fits the niche a congregation aspires to reach.

Methodist ministers vary not only in deciding how to dress. They also vary in choosing how to be addressed.

Ordained ministers in The United Methodist Church accept or claim a variety of titles that do not seem to correlate with their preferred worship settings or clothing styles. And they are so idiosyncratic that they cannot actually be considered signs or symbols of ordination. Terms such as *pastor* and *minister* and *preacher* are rather widely used to convey some sense of the functional role occupied by one who has been ordained and appointed. The term *reverend*, an adjective that has been elevated in general usage to the status of a title, offers a convenient way to greet or identify an ordained minister.

But so many words are used to express personal titles and ministerial actions that it is difficult to say United Methodists share a common vocabulary. One person who is appointed by the bishop may prefer to be known as Rev. Smith. The next appointee, holding an earned or honorary doctorate, may want to be called Dr. Jones. The person who is appointed after that may like a casual—but not completely casual—relationship and will ask to be called Pastor Jane. The appointment that follows might send an individual who values friendly, personal ties and who asks to be called Bob.

There is also no consistency in the language used to describe the duties, activities, and functions of persons in the ordained ministry. Some "preach," and the content of what they offer may be called a *sermon*. Others, sensitive to the pejorative connotation of being preachy and sermonic, say that they "deliver" the content of what they call *messages*. Unlike the technical jargon that may distinguish between *administering* the sacraments or *presiding* at the celebration of sacraments (terms that merit meaningful theological discussion but rarely have an impact on the perceived practices of ordained ministry), the words *preach* and *sermon* and *deliver* and *message* have been market tested. And in churches that are at least "market wise" if not "market driven," words are carefully chosen so as to attract participants and avoid repelling prospects.

The signs and symbols of ordained ministry in The United Methodist Church are a blend of sacred and secular images. For settled congregations in specific contexts, traditions have been established even by churches that would ardently insist that they are not bound by traditions. On several occasions, when I have been invited to be a guest preacher at United Methodist churches, the host pastor usually helps me understand the importance of knowing what to wear. For a so-called contemporary service, slacks and a shirt without a necktie are expected, although as a guest my necktie might be tolerated. For a so-called traditional service, a robe or alb and stole would be expected, although as a guest my business suit without a robe might be allowed.

Whatever one wears, one has to respect the context. In most African-American churches, the typical white-church–middle-class sermon lasting twenty minutes will be heard as if only half a loaf were served at a meal. Not only will the length and content of the sermon have to respect the setting, but also some space will have to be provided between words or within phrases for worshipers to respond in affirmations or encouragements.

There are classic, cultural, contextual issues that are as important to the ordained ministry of The United Methodist Church as are the theological understandings of ordination. There is a confusing mixture of sacred and secular, contextual and Christian, marketable and mysterious that has an impact on describing the ordained ministry for Methodism.

Several years ago, I directed a research project that included several facets, one of which was an assessment of the reasons why ordained ministers left the *pastoral ministry*. A major complicating factor was to define the term *pastoral ministry* in such a way that one could tell whether an individual had left it. Some cases were easily identified and obvious. If an ordained United Methodist took a job managing a toy store, that person clearly had left pastoral ministry. But if, after serving on the staff of a local church for several years following ordination, someone took a position managing an urban homeless shelter and running a food pantry, there could be a debate about whether that was a departure from pastoral ministry or an entry into a new form of it. One scholar who was conducting the research insisted that pastoral ministry actually meant being a pastor (or a member of a pastoral staff) at a local church. By that definition, all sorts of ordained ministers — bishops, district superintendents, military chaplains, hospital directors of pastoral care, prison ministers, and professors in schools of theology—would be deemed to have left pastoral ministry!

Yet the language in *The Book of Discipline of The United Methodist Church* could be interpreted to support such a perspective. For a few decades, ordained ministers who were appointed to chaplaincies, professorships, and campus ministries were labeled as being "appointed beyond the local church," signifying that the normative appointment for an ordained minister is to an existing congregation. Currently such appointments are called "extension ministries." The language today is a bit more hospitable to considering a hospice chaplain as a person engaged in pastoral ministry. But the terminology still seems to insist that the local church is the place for real ministry, and other settings offer exceptions to real ministry.

That distinction becomes an important symbol. John Wesley, after his ordination, served in only one local church or parish assignment for the rest of his life—when he assisted his father, Samuel, in the two communities of Epworth and Wroot. His other ministerial appointments included chaplain to the colonists (many of them refugees from debtors' prison) in Georgia, university professor, and self-appointed leader of a spiritual renewal movement that became known as Methodism. But in United Methodism, well into the twenty-first century, candidates for ordained ministry who express a sense of call to military chaplaincy, campus ministry, or academic scholarship are told they must spend a few years pastoring local churches before they can be approved for ordination. Such actions not only display an unnecessarily narrow view of the places where ordained ministers can legitimately serve; they also exhibit an inadequate understanding of the nature of ordination in the life of the church.

Manifesting the Mission of the Church

The signs of ordained ministry are not defined according to their public display in types of attire or forms of address or places of professional activity. The signs of ordained ministry are in the ways that they manifest the mission of the church. Deacons engage in ministries of the Word (e.g., teaching, preaching, writing, and counseling) and in ministries of service (e.g., conducting music, caring for children, calling upon the sick, comforting the bereaved, and calling groups of people together to address community needs for housing or justice or peace). Elders engage in such ministries of word and service, too, along with ministries of sacrament (presiding both at Holy Communion and at baptism) and order (presiding over conferences and congregations, and transforming organizational systems).

These are not simply the functions they perform. They are the symbols of the mission of the church.

What transforms a sign into a symbol is the way it actually participates in and conveys the power of what it signifies. Many people conduct music, care for children, call upon the sick, comfort the bereaved, and call people together to work for justice or peace. Those are noble and constructive acts of human decency, of civic virtue, of Christian witness. But when ordained deacons and elders engage in such actions, they are providing symbols that this is the mission of the church in the world. They are more than moral—and certainly more than political—actions. They are part of and participants in the will of God who sent the church of Jesus Christ into the world with a mission. Ordained ministers have been authorized by the church to engage in that mission.

Others can do it. Others may do it. Ordained ministers must do it because they are the symbols of God's will to redeem and to transform. When the world sees people engaged in the mission for which they have been ordained, the symbol will make God's saving grace self-evident. Perhaps a type of dress or a title of address helps signify that a missional symbol is present. But the symbol that inheres in the mission is what an ordained minister does in the art and action of word, service, sacrament, and order, not in what one wears or how one is labeled. Enhancing this symbolic power is the fact that ordained ministers in The United Methodist Church are sent into places of service as deacons and elders. They bring whatever assortment of gifts and grace God may have granted and they may have cultivated through education, prayer, and dedication. More important, they are sent by the authority of the connectional church as visible presence of the church's disciplined mission.

At the same time, there are subtle but significant differences between the sending of elders and the sending of deacons. Besides the different forms of ministry for which they are ordained, deacons and elders are sent under different patterns of appointment making. Deacons may initiate their own appointments by seeking and finding positions that are appropriate to their ordination, or the bishops and district superintendents may initiate conversations with deacons about appointment possibilities. Elders, too, may initiate contacts (e.g., with a hospital about becoming a director of pastoral care or with a theological school about becoming a dean), but they remain available "without reserve to be appointed and to serve, after consultation, as the appointive authority may determine" (*The Book of Discipline*, ¶ 333, p. 240).

These distinctions can have practical, professional, and financial implications. In the language of the denomination, deacons are full clergy members of their annual conferences but "are not guaranteed a place of employment in the church" (*The Book of Discipline*, ¶ 331.14c, p. 240), while elders are full clergy members of annual conferences who "are appointed by the bishop to fields of labor" through an "itinerant system" (*The Book of Discipline*, ¶ 338, p. 248), which guarantees that they "shall be continued under appointment by the bishop" (*The Book of Discipline*, ¶ 337.1, p. 247). Elders are appointed with the expectation that they will be appointed to full-time service, defined to mean that an elder's "entire vocational time . . . is devoted to the work of ministry in the field of labor to which one is appointed by the bishop" (*The Book of Discipline*, ¶ 338.1, p. 248). Only at the request of an elder may an appointment be made to less than full-time service. And, absent any such request, an elder who is a conference member in full connection is guaranteed to receive a salary that is "not less than base compensation established by the annual conference for persons in full-time service" (*The Book of*

Discipline, ¶ 342.1, p. 254). Should an elder request less than full-time service and should the bishop choose to honor that request, the compensation must be pro-rated according to the percentage of full-time and according to the minimum salary levels determined by the annual conference. Deacons, on the other hand, may be appointed "at their request or with their consent" to a position that offers no compensation, or they may seek and find a position of service but discover that the bishop "may choose not to make that appointment" (*The Book of Discipline,* ¶ 331.6c–d, p. 237). If a deacon is appointed to a full-time position in a local church or similar ecclesiastical setting, the deacon is assured of having the same claim as an elder on the compensation minimums established by the annual conference, unless that position is stipulated to be "nonsalaried" (*The Book of Discipline,* ¶ 331.14bc, p. 239).

Therefore, an elder in full connection is guaranteed to receive an appointment and to be paid a salary that does not drop below an established minimum, but the elder must be available to itinerate from one appointment to another. A deacon in full connection is neither guaranteed to receive an appointment nor to be assured of some minimum compensation, but she or he remains free to find settings that are appropriate to ordination. An elder could find himself or herself without a job and without a salary only by having requested some sort of leave from the itinerant ministry. Otherwise, every elder who is neither retired nor on leave is guaranteed a position by the church, unless some questionable conduct or chargeable offense has led to the elder's being put on suspension from the practice of ordained ministry pending some administrative or judicial review. A deacon could find himself or herself without a job and without a salary not only under the same conditions that apply to elders, but also under circumstances that involve failure to find a job, failure to secure a bishop's appointment to a job that one has found, or failure to find a job except for one that carries no compensation and consenting to accept an appointment to it. In summary, an elder has greater assurance of professional and financial security, but a deacon has greater freedom to determine professional placement. An elder must itinerate but will be paid. A deacon need not itinerate but may not be paid.

Complications of Authorizations

As I have said, at the General Conference in 1996, The United Methodist Church made the dramatic decision to shift from sequential ordinations of ministers as deacons and elders to separate orders of ministry as deacons and elders. The impact of this act upon individuals and implications for the institution are still unfolding. Deacons are not ordained to ministries of "order" in the life of the church, but as full clergy members of annual conferences they bear responsibilities identical to many (but not all) of the responsibilities of elders who are ordained to ministries of order. Deacons have greater financial vulnerability yet greater professional freedom than elders. Elders must meet certain educational requirements prior to being ordained, but not all of those requirements apply to deacons. An elder, for example, is required to earn a master of divinity degree or its equivalent. A deacon is required to earn a master's degree that may or may not be a theological degree; if it be in the field of theology, it does not have to meet a level of equivalency with the master of divinity (though some basic graduate studies in theological disciplines are required).

These and other complications are tremendously important for people who are already ordained as deacons and elders to understand as they collegially labor together in the mission of the church. They are also relevant for individuals who are in the process of considering their calls to ordained ministry. It will be vital for individuals to discern, as early as possible, the sense of vocation that beckons them toward the ordained ministry. Whether it will be in the ministry of elder or of deacon will play a role in the decisions made about their educational programs. The type of ordained ministry to which one feels called in the future will shape the education that one pursues in the present.

Moreover, the words and actions of authorization for ministry in an ordination service are important symbols. They symbolically exhibit how the ministries of deacon and elder express the nature and mission of the church. They symbolize the transforming power for which candidates are ordained and the transforming mandate they will exercise wherever they are appointed. This is not only a personal

matter to be appreciated by individuals who are approaching ordination. It is also an ecclesiastical matter to be
appreciated by the church under whose authorization they
are being ordained.

Their signs and symbols of ordination are often
confusing not only within the life of United Methodism
but also in the denomination's ecumenical partnerships
and public action. Everything that a deacon is authorized
by ordination to do can be done—and is generally expected
to be done—by laypeople. Some things that deacons are
not authorized by their ordination to do (e.g., participate in
ordering the life of the church), they actually do under their
status as clergy members of the annual conference. Some
authorizations that are granted by ordination only to elders
(e.g., presiding at the administration of the sacraments)
can be bestowed upon deacons merely by the consent of a
bishop (*The Book of Discipline*, ¶ 328, p, 231).

The United Methodist Church has recently been
engaged in bilateral conversations with Lutherans and Episcopalians. Among the considerations have been mutual
recognition of each other's ordained ministry and mutual
acceptance of shared fellowship at the Lord's Table for
Holy Communion. These relationships are terribly significant for United Methodists, who have consistently adopted
a positive ecumenical posture at all levels of church life—
local, regional, denominational, and global. Yet, since the
ordained ministry is a dimension of the church's life, the
church must assume responsibility for clearly articulating

the authorizations it grants to ordained ministers in providing leadership for the mission of the church. Otherwise it puts the individual deacon—who may have been granted sacramental authority by the consent of her or his bishop—in a compromised position. The deacon may not know whether to exercise that authority while conducting an ecumenical service at her or his local church. It also puts an individual bishop who may be assigned to an episcopal area where a predecessor bishop granted sacramental authority to a deacon but is not inclined to support continuation of that grant—for ecumenical or other reasons—in a similarly compromised position.

If there are important distinctions between the kinds of authority granted to different orders of ministry, those distinctions should be clearly established in the laws of the church as distinguishing marks of ordained ministry. If there is value in having two separate orders of ordained ministry, the authorizations that distinguish them should be clearly and precisely drawn. If there is no theologically coherent way to articulate the difference, then the church should consider simply having ordained "ministers" rather than ordained "deacons" and ordained "elders."

The ordained ministry can effectively communicate and authoritatively lead the mission of the church only if the church clearly establishes the signs and symbols that are intended to be bestowed by ordination. Otherwise, two intractable problems will be created. One is the loss of an ordained ministry as a disciplined, covenantal community carrying out the mission of the church. A second is the absence of any means to assess effectiveness in ministry, because it will have become impossible to know the standards of discipline against which assessments will be made. Unless the church knows what the signs and symbols of ordained ministry are, neither the church nor anyone in the public arena will recognize the presence of Christian mission when it appears.

CHAPTER 6

Exiting from Ordained Ministry

As the campaign for the 1988 presidential election in the United States got underway, two of the more interesting candidates were Pat Robertson and Jesse Jackson. Both had been ordained as Baptist ministers. But beyond that formal similarity, they had little in common.

Robertson had become an influential public figure through his television program, *The 700 Club*, and his cable television company, CBN (Christian Broadcasting Network). He founded a number of political, religious, and service ventures, including Regent University in Virginia Beach. Ideologically identified with strongly conservative or right-wing perspectives and nominally a Republican, he had moved theologically away from the textually based biblical authority that is most typical of the Southern Baptists by whom he had been ordained and toward a more charismatic approach.

Jackson had become a well-known public figure from his days as a colleague with Martin Luther King Jr., in the struggle for the civil rights of African Americans. Building upon his base of support within the community of left-leaning activists as well as his connections with the black church, Jackson was an active Democrat who had developed a network of organizations devoted to community service and public lobbying such as Operation Push. Because he was frequently available for media interviews and because he presented himself as a resource to help solve various crises, he managed to be visible nationally and internationally.

During the early primary phase of the presidential campaign, both Robertson and Jackson seemed to arouse a lot more attention than votes. Neither had a realistic chance of winning a major party nomination or of making a significant impact on the race by running as an Independent. But they both made news, including the occasion when Robertson announced that he was withdrawing from the ordained ministry not only because he valued the separation of church and state, but also because he felt called to public service as a national political leader rather than to ordained ministry. Jackson responded that, in the tradition from which he came, such a departure from the ordained ministry was impossible. In Jackson's view, when God calls a person, that person stays called.

But in fact both Robertson and Jackson had stayed active in the ordained ministry only if one indulges in a very generous definition of ordained ministry. Their spat raises a debatable point about the call to ordained ministry. One can legitimately wonder whether a person who is called will always remain called. One may ponder, after someone enters ordained ministry, what may be involved in exiting from ordained ministry—or if such a thing is even possible.

There are theological traditions within Christianity that believe ordination fundamentally alters the nature of the human being who is ordained. In this view, certain indelible traits are granted to and are imposed upon the individual ordinand. To withdraw from ordained ministry a system with that understanding would require the removal of whatever has been added to the human character.

The act of ordination in United Methodism's theological understanding, however, does not confer upon the ordinand some alteration in human nature. Nor does ordination grant to the individual some set of entitlements that become the ordinand's possession. To be ordained is to be received into an order of the church, to be yoked with specific covenantal relationships, and to be provided with authorizations from the church for fulfilling certain responsibilities. Yet the authority that is granted in ordination remains the prerogative and the property of the church for the purpose of the church's mission.

A Mantle Worn but Not Owned

To be ordained deacon or elder is to enter an order of ministry in the church. The church shares specific missional authority with the ordinand. Nevertheless, that authority resides with the church. It is not a trophy that an individual permanently takes home. It is a mantle that the church permits a person to wear but never to own.

Methodism has adapted a variety of terms to describe this understanding. For a time, late in the twentieth century, United Methodists spoke of ordination in terms of *representative* ministry. This evocative approach conveyed a sense that ordained ministers *represented God to the church* through the proclamation of the Word and the administration of the sacraments; that they *represented the church to God* in prayers, liturgies, disciplined lives of devotion, along with other practices; and that they *represented the church to the world* through acts of service. Later the concept of representative ministry was set aside and succeeded by servant leadership (*The Book of Discipline*, ¶¶ 132–138, pp. 91–93), a phrase that seemed conventional in the corporate world and translated well into the ecclesiastical world.

In seeking to use such phrases, the church has groped for language to cultivate a carefully nuanced pattern of awareness. First, everyone who is baptized into the community of faith should feel summoned both to serve and to lead. Second, ordained ministers are a called cohort of individuals within the life of the church who commit to every aspect of Christian mission and discipline that is expected of all Christians but who are granted specific authority for certain forms of serving and leading. Third, the church authorizes ordained ministers to engage in particular types of serving and leading on behalf of the church. Ministers know that they receive the authorizations for which they are especially suited by their gifts and that they will be more vigorously held accountable by the church because of the authority that has been entrusted to them.

Just as the language in vogue may influence the terms used for describing ministerial roles (e.g., *representative ministry* and *servant leadership*), vocabulary can shift based on the way ordained ministers are viewed in relationship to other professionals.

Sometimes the choice of vocabulary leans strongly to the sacred, as if to distinguish the church from the world. Words such as *pastor* and *homily* are almost exclusively internal to the life of the church; when they apply to the roles and responsibilities of ordained ministers, they emphasize the ways in which the church is different or separated from the world. At other times, a choice of vocabulary and imagery that borrows heavily from the secular may intend to show how the church connects with the world. An elder who is appointed to a local church with responsibility for maintaining its order and discipline could be understood as fulfilling the ministry of her or his ordination and be called the minister of order. But such a title would almost certainly be rejected in preference for a title such as executive pastor. The church can readily accommodate itself to the concept of an "executive" in ministry. But it cannot so easily explain to its own constituents and to the world that "order" is a legitimate (and indeed essential) aspect of the church's need for the ministry of an ordained elder.

The phrase *servant leadership* has found a place both in secular and sacred realms. It certainly resonates with the authorizations granted to deacons and elders in their ordinations. To serve is a responsibility of all Christians. And to *lead* is an expectation for all Christians, lay and ordained. To engage in servant leadership (something that is assumed as a task for every individual who holds membership in the church) is to be specifically entrusted by the church with an assigned authority by ordination. Deacons and elders "are called by God to a lifetime of servant leadership in specialized ministries" and are to exhibit a "faithful commitment to servant leadership" throughout their lives (*The Book of Discipline*, ¶ 138, p. 93).

A Call in Question

Yet everyone can cite examples where something has gone awry with that call. There may be some form of gross misconduct by an ordained minister, perhaps even involving criminal charges. There may be evidence—apparent to the ordained minister, to the persons among whom one engages in ministry, and/or to those who supervise ordained ministers in their professional activities—that the individual's practice of ministry has become unsatisfying or ineffective. There may be an opportunity to pursue some very fulfilling form of work that is not suitable as a ministerial appointment. Several decades ago, for example, an ordained United Methodist launched a campaign for election to a seat in Congress. When he won, his bishop faced a dilemma, for there was no provision in the church's *Book of Discipline* that permitted a bishop to appoint someone to the House of Representatives.

The most highly publicized situations involving ordained ministers are typically those associated with scandalous behavior. While sexual abuse of young parishioners by Roman Catholic priests has been the dominant example of such misconduct in recent years, United Methodists have also faced allegations of inappropriate sexual, financial, and criminal activities. There are clearly defined procedures in The United Methodist Church for submitting, processing, and adjudicating complaints or charges against an ordained minister (*Book of Discipline*, ¶ 361, pp. 283–86). One possible path is for the accused to withdraw from the ordained ministry, stipulating that the withdrawal is "under complaint" or "under charges" (*The Book of Discipline*, ¶360.3, pp. 282–83). Another possible path can lead to a church trial, which can be claimed as a constitutional right by any member of the church, ordained or lay (*The Book of Discipline*, ¶ 20, p. 27).

These involve the most extreme situations. Even at their extremity, they illustrate a key point about the nature of the call to ordained ministry. It is both inward and outward (*The Book of Discipline*, ¶ 137, p. 92). An individual may be the one to begin questioning whether he or she is still "called." The church may initiate the questioning whether an ordained minister is still "called." For a call to be valid prior to ordination, both the inward and outward dimensions of call must be present. For a call to be validly judged to have lapsed, both inward and outward discernments must be made.

For that reason, the church has provided a number of forms of "leave" and "location" that can be used to address temporary or permanent circumstances in life without having to determine that the call has died or that it was erroneously judged to have been present in the first place. One may remain in the ordained ministry but seek leave from it for a period of time to care for personal or family needs, to take maternity or paternity leave, and to deal with medical issues or disabling conditions. One can remain in the ordained ministry but take a sabbatical leave for some time to study or travel. One can remain in the ordained ministry but decide no longer to be in the itinerant ministry and seek honorable location of the individual's orders. None of these involves discernment about the loss of call.

The most challenging and difficult circumstances of discernment are not matters of temporary leave from the practice of ministry or permanent location from itinerant ministry. They are not even those painful and heartbreaking processes involving complaints or charges about moral misconduct by ordained ministers, as troubling as they may be.

The toughest tasks are in discerning how to deal with chronic ineffectiveness, deep dissatisfaction, and a deficiency of spiritual fulfillment. Such things may have been observed by those who supervise ordained ministers, identified by those who are in the communities to be served by ordained ministers, or felt by ordained ministers themselves who cannot determine what to do about those feelings.

There are persons who, years or even decades after ordination, have to be told that their journeys as servant leaders in the mission of the church are demonstrating neither fruitful nor effective achievements. There are persons who look into the mirrors of their ministries and face the fact that trying to serve professionally in the name of the Redeemer is no longer—if it ever was—a redemptive way for them to spend a life.

Discernment and Process

Like any discernment about the presence of a call, the discernment about the absence or loss of a call must include both inward and outward judgments. At the beginning of the process, an individual cannot make authentic self-determinations about whether a feeling of being called is genuinely the movement of the Holy Spirit or merely the rush of emotion. At a later turning point, such as consideration about exiting from ordained ministry, one cannot make a self-authenticating choice based solely on inward feelings. At every point in the process, the church has to make its assessments about the outward facets of a call appropriately, not reducing them to the most readily available data or suppressing the evidence that the gifts associated with a call have waned or died. The issues are different from questions about some possible change in appointment; they go to the heart and soul of ordained ministry itself.

During the early days of Methodism, John and Charles Wesley argued about a man who had been a tailor but was appointed as a preacher. The brothers debated whether, by the grace of God, the tailor had become a preacher or, by the grace of God, he had been restored to his proper life as a tailor.

Compassion and mercy obligate the church to ensure that ordained ministers in the midst of vocational crises be shown respect, care, and support. The mission that provides the foundation for the ordained ministry obligates the church to ensure that none of its ordained ministers be permitted to forsake vocational clarity merely to keep a job, an income, or a status. Mediocrity must not be a chargeable offense against the church nor an acceptable performance standard by ordained ministers within the church.

Legislatively, in the coming years, The United Methodist Church will consider amending the church law that says that "elders in full connection . . . shall be continued under appointment by the bishop" which in effect guarantees a place of service and a minimum salary to all elders from the moment of their ordination until the mandate of their retirements (*The Book of Discipline*, ¶ 337.1, p. 247).

The incentives for making such a change are strong. A perception exists that many ordained elders are persistently ineffective and professionally hard to appoint yet impossible to set aside from the itinerancy until they retire or unless they commit some grievous offense. A perception exists that a number of these persons are impeding the vitality of the church because they are preventing spiritually energetic persons from entering the itinerant ministry. A perception exists that until bishops and annual conferences, through their cabinets and their boards of ordained ministry respectively, can be liberated from the constraints imposed by this guarantee of appointment, the work of the Holy Spirit to fulfill the mission of the church will be impaired.

It may be necessary to modify the law of the church on this matter, if only to liberate the church from the uncertainty about whether these perceptions are true. Once the guarantee of an appointment is removed from the law of the church, bishops and annual conferences (through their respective cabinets and boards of ordained ministry) will have to develop with great rigor and great grace the instruments of assessment that determine genuine missional effectiveness. Then the ordained ministers (deacons and elders) will know what the actual measurements of effectiveness are, because the members of the annual conferences will be writing them. Then the mission of the church will be translated into language that clergy and laity will be able to recognize as the mandate of Christ against which faithfulness in discipleship will be assessed. Then the people of The United Methodist Church will see more clearly what kinds of gifts and what forms of grace should be present in persons whom they might scout as possible candidates for ordained ministry. Then the boards of ordained ministry will be able to weigh with merit that equals psychological testing, criminal background checks, academic transcripts, and incidental sermons, the array of gifts that every candidate will bring to the ministry for advancing the mission of the church.

Liberated from an artificial and inequitable guarantee of appointment, the ordained ministry of United Methodism will be forced to the truly challenging question. No longer will there be an excuse to rely upon a perception that the church has too many ineffective ministers. The church will have to define—clearly, unambiguously and missionally—what constitutes effective ministry. Then the church will have to describe how to apply the standards established for effectiveness, knowing that the results achieved will be those for which programs of assessment are drawn.

Standardized testing has become a common feature to identify the achievement levels of public schools, to project the performance of future college students, and to determine who will constitute the pool of potential recruits for police work or firefighting or safe driving. While such instruments have a demonstrated value in offering one way to measure present accomplishment or potential for success, they have a serious limitation in that they ultimately measure only one thing—the ability to take a standardized test.

If the church decides that measuring congregational worship attendance is the best way to assess the relative effectiveness of ordained ministry, then ministers will find ways to pack the pews with people. If the church decides that improving the high school graduation rate in the communities where they serve is integral to Christian mission, then ordained ministers will collectively find ways to connect with public and private education. If the church decides that improving public health must be measured as part of the mission of the church, then ordained ministers under appointment will open clinics and invest other resources in enhancing the well-being of the communities where they are sent. If the church decides that providing seed money for grants to establish emerging congregations in economically deprived but missionally vital neighborhoods is a prophetic witness of the Holy Spirit, then ordained ministers will discover creatively how to help new communities of faith to emerge.

Along the way, some ordained ministers will discover that they do not believe that such things are essential to the mission of the church or that they do not have the gifts to provide leadership for such elements of the mission. They will initiate their own exits from the ordained ministry, or the persons who superintend them will start the proceedings to help them see the merits of transitioning to other careers. Their departures will be for the cause of the Christian mission. And the rise of new candidates for ordained ministry will be a response to that mission as well.

As challenging as these processes may be, even more difficult ones might develop in time. The church may have to imagine changing some other legislation, such as the laws that address the effectiveness of bishops. Elections to the episcopacy in recent years have tended to focus on making sure that a representative presence is maintained in the Council of Bishops and that signs of executive leadership in an individual bishop are suitably matched with the needs for episcopal leadership in a given area. Assignments of bishops to their respective episcopal areas by the jurisdictional committees on episcopacy have tended to privilege the notion that a bishop will be the chief executive officer of an annual conference. The church needs a more missional perspective on the selections and assignments of its bishops. The church also needs a more missional system for retaining bishops in their work.

But, under current church law, bishops are elected for a lifetime. Only a decision to resign the office or retire prematurely from the office, or a judicial proceeding about some form of misconduct, can lead to a bishop's removal from office before mandated retirement. If the church chooses to eliminate a guarantee of appointment for ordained elders in itinerant ministry, it seems reasonable that the church could also choose to eliminate a lifetime guarantee of place for those individuals in the itinerant general superintendency. Procedures for helping ineffective ministers to exit from ordained ministry should not be reserved for those who are under appointment but should be provided for those making the appointments as well.

CHAPTER 7

Preparing for Ordained Ministry

In the twenty-first century, the ordained ministry is undergoing a radical transition. What it will be in the coming decades is not yet clear. But one immensely important anniversary to be marked in 2017 may offer a hint about how powerfully such changes can transform the church and its ministries.

October 31, 2017, marks the five-hundredth anniversary of the start of the Protestant Reformation. On October 31, 1517, when Martin Luther posted a notice on a church door in Wittenberg inviting church leaders and scholars to a public debate on ninety-five propositions concerning theology, ecclesiology, sacraments, and ministry, no one could have foreseen the ensuing events, changing world history to this day. Even if we consider just a few elements of one facet of the Reformation—namely, the changes in ordained ministry—the impact was enormous. Luther challenged the principle that ordained persons controlled a sacramental system that in turn had sole control over access to salvation. He insisted that clergy be called to their places of service by the congregations among whom they ministered rather than be named to positions for which they had priestly oversight, no matter how infrequently they actually visited or provided ministry in those settings. He proposed that the preaching of the Word was actually a means for taking the written word of the Bible and restoring it to its original, pristine form—its oral form—through proclamation under the guidance of the Holy Spirit.

Simply put, the year 2017 marks the five-hundredth anniversary of launching a revolution in understanding the ordained ministry of the church. And it was not simply a debate between the established Roman Catholic Church in Europe and the Protestants who protested against official church patterns. It quickly developed into intense debates among the Protestant Reformers over matters such as the nature of the sacraments that the church celebrated and the authority of the ordained ministers who presided over them. Protestants argued among themselves whether baptism brought about some objective change in the life of the individual receiving the water or brought that individual into the community of faith where God's grace could become a living promise in the life of a church member. They debated among themselves: did the words and actions used by the ordained person who presided in administering the sacraments have the real power to accomplish the work of God's grace, or did the faith of the individual matter in the act of receiving God's grace through the sacraments? They fought—sometimes with fatal consequences—about the legitimacy of administering baptism as a sign of God's promise to an infant versus the necessity of reserving baptism for persons old enough or mature enough to make a confession of faith.

Battles raged. Theologians debated. Clergy and laity died at the hands of other clergy and laity. Real estate and other valuable property changed hands. Church buildings were destroyed or severely damaged. Books were written. Books were banned. Books were burned. Principalities, powers, states, and empires went to war. Missions were launched. Music was composed. Choirs sang works of great beauty. Partisans wrote works of great animosity. Love was celebrated. Hate was elevated.

And ordained ministry was redefined in countless ways, as it has been continually and remarkably redefined in the five centuries since Martin Luther—a thirty-four-year-old priest and biblical theologian—posted his propositions for debate on a church door in Germany. Methodism did not emerge as a movement founded upon a Wesleyan theological perspective until centuries after Luther's death. Ordained ministry became part of the Methodist movement only decades after that. And in the centuries since, the ordained ministry in Methodism has continued to change, evolve, and be transformed.

Between the five-hundredth anniversary of the start of the Protestant Reformation in 2017 and the three-hundredth anniversary of the first Methodist conference in 2044, many aspects of ordained ministry in Methodism may acquire new and clearer contours. Whether The United Methodist Church will endure as a denomination is still to be determined. Whether individuals will have to answer Wesley's historic questions before becoming ordained ministers is unknown. Whether the ordained ministry will endure as a way to offer to Methodists a career path for thousands of full-time professionals remains uncertain. Whether assessments and evaluations of Methodists seeking to enter ordained ministry will be made by a covenanted conference, a collection of independent congregations, an order of preachers, or some other entity will have to be decided.

Only the events of the coming decades and the historians who examine them will clarify the nature and the radical qualities of the transitions now occurring in ordained ministry. In the meantime, we labor on while circumstances and systems are changing in such uncertain ways. Any Methodist who is pondering a call to ordained ministry—either inwardly as a personal discernment or outwardly as an ecclesiastical discernment about other people who may have the gifts and grace—has some choices to make without knowing even the general direction of future transitions. It is vital, in this vacuum of any assurance, to make risky decisions about preparing for ordained ministry.

First, ordained ministry in Methodism is not fundamentally a matter of institutional security. Ordained ministry in Methodism is about commitment to a mission that: insists on the evangelical unity of personal and social holiness; preaches salvation as the work of God's grace affirmed by people of faith through their beliefs and practices; celebrates God's grace through sacramental actions that properly exhibit both the promises of God and the disciplines of life; devotes every resource to spreading scriptural holiness among people and reforming the world.

The United Methodist Church may continue to adapt and endure, but it may continue also to falter and fragment. Ordained ministry in The United Methodist Church does not exist simply to populate, perpetuate, or prop up an institution. Ordained ministry in United Methodism exists for the purpose of a mission. An institutionalized or organized denomination is one way to move that mission from concept to action. And the various branches of Methodist life have done that, more or less effectively, for hundreds of years. Nevertheless, the denomination does not determine the mission. The mission has to define—and ultimately determine the viability of—a denomination.

In that sense, the ordained ministry has the great privilege and even greater responsibility to function as a prophetic voice within the church. Precisely because ordained ministers are sent like apostles into the world, ordained ministers must periodically look, from the perspective of the world, at the church and ask whether the

Christian community is adhering to its own mission. Ordained ministers are representatives in many senses. Among them are the ways in which they represent the church to the world as apostles of the church's mission. Ordained ministers are not representatives of the institution but of the mission.

Therefore, in preparing for ordained ministry, the first step is to become involved in the missional purpose for which the church exists. Christians in other parts of the world teach us that this can mean becoming involved in three forms of activity: participating in a worshiping community, engaging in the education of young people (children and youth), and investing oneself in some social or civic action for the transformation of the world's systems (e.g., health, justice, or liberation from some addiction). Becoming active in Christian mission is the best way to begin a process of discernment—inwardly and outwardly—about the signs of the presence of a call to ordained ministry.

A second step in preparing for ordained ministry is to verbalize a sense that a call *may* be present. Too many people in the church have been reticent to participate in the *outward* aspect of the call by approaching someone, especially a young person, and raising the possibility that God may be calling that person to ordained ministry. Too many people in the church have been reluctant to initiate a conversation with a pastor, parent, spouse, or someone else and express the *inward* feeling of being called by God to ordained ministry. Either step is appropriately preliminary, and either one can be taken prior to the other. Neither is definitive, decisive, nor dangerous. Both can result from inward experiences that emerge from involvement in the church's mission or outward observations that can be made about involvement in the church's mission.

This step, taken as early as possible, can open an essential vocational pathway toward an eventual decision. On the one hand, the only way to engage in personal reflection that is truly honest is to acknowledge one's curiosity and uncertainty about the possibility that God is beckoning. On the other hand, the only way to have those feelings and those reflections assessed is by permitting an external word to be heard.

A third step in preparing for ordained ministry is to examine in reasonable depth the forms of ordained ministry into which persons are sent. Some are parochial (within the local church, congregation, or parish), and others are public (within community organizations or agencies for social service). Some are within ecclesiastical institutions (pastors and liturgists); others are within nonecclesiastical institutions (military chaplains and prison ministers). Some require very specialized talent and training (church music directors and medical missionaries); others require more generalized talent and training (ministers who visit people who are confined to home or who reside in skilled nursing centers). Some serve in complex organizations where they manage other highly skilled professionals or substantial resources (including funds and facilities); others serve in single-cell organizations where they manage people who volunteer for tasks that demand no special skills. Some spend many years to be trained as scholars in highly refined intellectual disciplines; others spend far less time but bring no less talent to engage in highly randomized social interactions.

Preparing for ordained ministry involves exploring many forms of ordained ministry, if only to recognize that the most visible of them are not the only kinds available. At the same time, preparing for ordained ministry includes respecting the fact that not every form of human activity is a form of ordained ministry—despite certain outward similarities. There are some very famous people in the United States and in other parts of the world who adapt certain features of church life and claim that they are engaged in ministry. It is important to remember that just because someone stands in front of a large or small group of people and delivers a mesmerizing or motivating talk does not mean that he or she is engaged in ministry—let alone ordained ministry. Both inward and outward aspects of a call are essential to discern that some form of endeavor actually is within the ordained ministry of the church. And the endeavor, regardless of its success at drawing a crowd or raising money or filling a large building, is ordained ministry only if it expresses the mission of the church and fulfills one or more authorizations on behalf of the mission of the church. For the individual to claim inwardly that she or he is called by God to a marvelous ministry is not enough.

It is not a call unless outwardly the community of faith discerns it, too.

That discernment requires focusing on the authorizations that ordained ministers are given by ordination. For deacons, those are authorizations to teach or preach the Word and to serve. For elders, the authorizations are those two forms of ministry—word and service—and two others: presiding at the sacraments and ordering the life of the church. Efforts to discern inwardly and outwardly that a call to the ordained ministry is indeed present will require evidence of gifts and effectiveness in ministering to the church and the world with those gifts. An individual may have other talents, skills, and gifts. But it is the gifts for these ministries that must be known and shown.

Preparing for the ministry of deacon or elder requires both the intellectual and spiritual education necessary to achieve some level of mastery in knowing the content of the Word of God and some level of effectiveness in communicating the content of the Word of God. It is not simply a matter of knowing about the Bible or about the things that others have said about the Bible. Nor is it simply a matter of being glib, persuasive, thoughtful, or emotional in delivering messages—written, oral, or artistic—about the Word of the Lord. To prepare for ordination that authorizes one to conduct the ministry of a deacon or an elder is to master the theological content of God's Word: revealed in Scripture, articulated in multiple approaches to systematic theological expression, developed in structures that describe a Christian ethic, framed throughout Christian history in a variety of cultures and through an array of crises, manifest in practices of disciplined Christian living. To prepare for ordained ministry is to acquire an assortment of oral, written, and visual skills for communicating that content. Such things are essential to the mission of the church and, hence, mandatory for the ordained ministry.

Preparing for the ministry of deacon or elder also requires the intellectual and spiritual endeavors necessary to determine that one will thrive and feel fulfilled by engaging in a life of service. The specific forms of service in which one will be most fruitfully engaged can be determined at a later phase of the process. Whatever it is, however, that form of service will have to be something that is embraced by the mission of the church. One might serve, as a deacon or elder, in a ministry of counseling with those who have an addiction to gambling. But one would not serve, as a deacon or elder, in dealing blackjack at a casino. Moreover, it will have to be satisfying not only for the mission of the church but also for the soul of the individual. Pastoral counseling with addicted persons is something significantly needed in a world afflicted with multiple kinds of addictions. But it is extremely demanding work and, unless one finds it to be a spiritually fulfilling ministry, it could erode the soul of even the most dedicated servant.

Preparing for the ministry of elder additionally requires having the gifts and acquiring the skills needed to preside at sacraments. To preside is more than merely to take a prominent position at the font or the table of the Lord and pronounce powerful words while engaging in physical actions. Presiding includes enabling the church to grow in the depth of its spiritual experience while sharing the sacraments. Presiding further includes enabling the church to broaden its knowledge of the diverse understandings of grace that have been conveyed to the church through baptism and Holy Communion.

Finally, preparing for the ministry of elder requires identifying and employing the things that will be necessary to lead the church through its order and discipline. These are not matters of administrative competence alone, although managerial skills will certainly need to be present by talent or acquired by learning. A gift for ordering the church will have to be demonstrated by leading. Ordering the church whose mission includes discipling individuals and transforming the world will require involvement on many fronts—identifying and training volunteers; grasping the demographics of a community; offering a public voice in circumstances that call for prophetic action; maintaining a spiritual restraint when vengeful responses to criticism might be instinctive; recognizing that the church is not only the instrument of God's mission in the world but a human institution with budgets to manage and buildings to maintain according to the standards of law in the world. Ordering the church will involve clarity about whom to hire, courage about whom to fire, and capacity to do both with grace. Ordering the church will also involve the difficult work of discernment, when someone emerges with an inward claim of being called to ordained ministry while persuasive signs of the outward call—by every spiritual judgment—are absent.

Preparing for the ordained ministry will also necessitate the kind of formal education that suitably equips one for a life of fruitful accomplishment in these missional responsibilities. A commitment to education, including higher education, has been evident throughout Methodist life. One of John Wesley's early missionary acts was to found a school. One of the first decisions made by Bishop Coke and Bishop Asbury was to found a college. Throughout the years, Methodists have established more institutions for higher education in America than any other group, except possibly Roman Catholics (who constitute a far larger church).

At an important point in the middle of the nineteenth century, American Methodism began to wrestle with the fact that the laity in the church was becoming better educated than its clergy. People in the pews sensed they were asking tougher questions than the clergy seemed able—or willing—to address. As a result of that instinct, the church embarked upon a program of strengthening theological education for ordained ministry. Seminaries, schools of theology, and schools of divinity were founded to serve this perceived need.

Many of the institutions founded and funded by the Methodist laity remain in service to the church today. Yet educational preparation takes its place among the many transitions occurring in ordained ministry. Some units in the church—from small-membership congregations that imagine themselves with minimal needs for a pastoral leader to large-membership congregations that seem willing to hire program specialists for positions in ministry— seem ready to reduce the intellectual standards required for ordained or unordained professionals. Some individuals and groups in the church are willing to have an educated cohort of ordained ministers but prefer that the education be achieved in the cheapest, closest, and most convenient way possible. They are willing to settle for an assortment of courses taken online, classes taken in a random array of short-term intensive experiences, or readings completed without a critical analysis of what has been read.

Would such an education be adequate? In the twenty-first century, the need for a more widely educated constituency of ordained ministers is greater than ever before. Preparing for ordination now means getting ready to preach the Word, engage in service, preside at sacraments, and order the community of faith in a global context. Wherever an ordained minister is sent, the people among whom she or he serves will be those who encounter the world— affected by a global economy, impacted by immigration from numerous nations, enrolled in public schools with children and youth who come from different religious traditions as well as from backgrounds devoid of any religious practice. In the twenty-first century, ordained ministers will need to be prepared with sharply honed skills in critical theological reflection for the world into which they are sent. That world will pose challenging questions for which superficial or sentimental answers will not suffice. What's more, most who raise such hard issues or ask such tough questions will come armed with "knowledge" that they have quickly and easily obtained from electronic media. Ordained ministers in the twenty-first century will have to be able, critically and constructively, to recognize misinformation or disinformation where it is present and to offer thoughtful as well as faithful Christian insights.

Preparing for ordained ministry means preparing to encounter the people living in and sojourning through and the places where one will be apostolically sent. They deserve no less from the church than to have ordained ministers who are sent, prepared, to offer the truth. After all, it is only the truth that will set them free.

Index

CPSIA information can be obtained at www.ICGtesting.com
Printed in the USA
LVOW121900070213

319146LV00001B/231/P